ABOVE SCORCHED SKIES

A Story of Modern Warfare and World Power

ZACHARY S. DAVIS

Lawrence Livermore National Laboratory
Center for Global Security Research

Table of Contents

Prologue   Why is a nuclear weapons laboratory   i

publishing a work of fiction?

Dedication   iii

Acknowledgments   iv

Chapter One   Scorched Earth at the Top of the World   i

Chapter Two   The Gray Zone Beyond the Battlefield   9

Chapter Three   Escalation Without Off Ramps   16

Chapter Four   Crowded, Contested and Chaotic   31

Chapter Five   Carissa's Wargame   41

Chapter Six   Who Makes the Rules?   52

Chapter Seven   War In Space   59

Chapter Eight   Space in War   68

Chapter Nine   The Fog of War   75

Chapter Ten   The Dark Side of the Moon   79

Chapter Eleven   Children of Light and Children of   87

Darkness

TABLE OF CONTENTS

Chapter	Twelve	Throw a Coat Over It and Smack It With a Hammer	95
Chapter	Thirteen	Red Dawn	99
Chapter	Fourteen	Clausewitz in Space	104
Chapter	Fifteen	We're Going to Need A Bigger Boat	114
Chapter	Sixteen	Quicksilver Messenger Service	121
Chapter	Seventeen	Lucky's Covert Action	129
Chapter	Eighteen	Girl Power	132
Chapter	Nineteen	With a Little Help from My Friends	137
Chapter	Twenty	The Red Sparrow	139
Chapter	Twenty – One	My Dinner with Andrei	142
Chapter	Twenty – Two	Games Without Frontiers	145
Chapter	Twenty – Three	Revenge of the Nerds	148
Chapter	Twenty – Four	Friends in High Places	152
Chapter	Twenty – Five	The Tao of Physics	155
Chapter	Twenty – Six	The Smoore Flow	163
Chapter	Twenty – Seven	Mission Creep	166
Chapter	Twenty – Eight n	Space Diplomacy	170
Chapter	Twenty – Nine	The Anarchic Society	177

Chapter Thirty	Dharma Bums	185
Chapter Thirty One	Space Is the Place	192
Chapter Thirty – Two	Harvest for the World	199
Chapter Thirty – Three	Complex Deterrence and the Nth-Body Problem	205
Chapter Thirty – Four	Spies Like US	212
Chapter Thirty – Five	From Russia with Love	220
Chapter Thirty – Six	The Hotwash	226
Chapter Thirty – Seven	The Turning Point	236
Chapter Thirty - Eight	Keep on Rocking in the Free World	244
About the Author		250

Prologue: Why is a nuclear weapons laboratory publishing a work of fiction?

The Fourth Industrial Revolution is reshaping our world faster than we can adapt to the changes. Technology is outpacing our ability to develop policies to guide and govern the effects on society. Nowhere are these changes more revolutionary than in the realm of national security, where emerging technologies are changing the face of war and conflict. We see the outlines of the future in the uses of drones, autonomous vehicles, information, artificial intelligence, cyber, and space on the battlefield.

Our previous books on Strategic Latency provided a preview of what's coming, but we're not there yet. We have not yet completed the transition from our legacy systems of defense and deterrence to the arsenals of tomorrow. The result is a combination of old and new technologies stitched together in a prototype of the future force structures that we see forming on the horizon. This book imagines a war with both ancient and futuristic characteristics.

One of the most prominent features of the Fourth Industrial Revolution is the role of space. In recent years, we have become quietly dependent on space for nearly every aspect of our military, economic and social existence. The space domain is essential for navigation, communications, maneuver, targeting, intelligence, surveillance, and reconnaissance (ISR), and strategic deterrence. Beyond the military, so much of the global economy depends on space that it is worth asking what would happen if the entire space architecture disappeared overnight.

This book offers a fictional account of a war that escalates from the land and sea domains into the space domain. The story extrapolates from current political, military, and technological realities to portray a plausible, near-term future conflict. It is not supposed to be a completely accurate depiction of people, places, or things, and I have taken liberties that informed readers are likely to notice. This includes the technologies, institutions, and people who make up our national security enterprise. The goal is to stimulate discussion about the ways that technology is shaping national and international security and how we can work together to achieve our common objectives. Your suspension of disbelief about certain specifics will facilitate those discussions.

Still, you might be wondering why a national laboratory would produce a work of fiction. Lawrence Livermore National Lab (LLNL) and its sister labs are deeply involved in the exploration of new technologies. Our mission is to understand the cutting edge of science and technology and their applications to national security. At LLNL, the Center for Global Security Research (CGSR) examines the intersection of technology and policy and the implications of technology for defense and deterrence. This book weaves together many of the themes that we study – technology, deterrence, nuclear strategy, strategic latency, theories of victory, over-the-horizon threats, and multi-domain warfare -- into a story that we hope stimulates discussion. I wrote it in the spirit of what our colleague Peter Singer calls "useful fiction," stories that make us think about the path we are on and where it might lead. That's our job. I hope you like it.

Dedication

For those who serve

Acknowledgments

I threw everything but the kitchen sink into this book. The story includes themes of science and technology, geopolitics, regional studies, intelligence, deterrence, special operations, multi-domain warfare, policy, and bureaucracy. The stories and characters are based on my thirty-four years working for the US Government on national security issues. My knowledge about these topics comes from my colleagues who have devoted their lives to national service. The book is dedicated to those patriots who serve our county. I am in awe of their contributions and their commitment to keeping us safe and prosperous.

A few of those people should be recognized for their contributions to this project. My boss at CGSR, Brad Roberts, asked me, "Is that really what you want to do?" and gave me enough rope to hang myself. His deputy, Mike Albertson, read every draft and did his best to make it readable and relevant to our mission. CGSR researcher Thomas Von Bibber provided good comments on an early draft. Katie Thomas keeps me sane with her common sense and Warriors commentary.

My other boss at LLNL, Brad Hart, also allowed me to spend my time making up stories instead of doing real work. I hope he doesn't get in trouble. Adam Radin and his group provided insights into escalation in South Asia. Jerry Mullins makes everyone smarter. Ben Bahney and the space experts at LLNL nodded and gestured to keep me going in the right direction, but obviously didn't stop me from embarrassing myself. The CT group members asked if there are sex scenes in the book. Carissa would be proud of them.

Also at the lab, Kristine Wong, Cat Lee, Tom Reason and Kirk Hadley in the Technical Information Department worked their magic to produce a different sort of publication than our usual scientific and strategic policy publications.

The idea for the book came from George du Mais from the National Reconnaissance Office. George wrote a pathbreaking chapter for our last Strategic Latency book and recommended we focus the next one on space. George explained that we have lots of plans for a war in space but few ideas about what would happen in space during a big global war. That's where the idea of a ground war that migrates into space and wipes out everything in LEO originated.

My partner in strategic latency research, Frank Gac from Los Alamos lab, is the kindest, most genuine, and thoughtful person I know. That said, when I told him I didn't want to write another book, he reassured me that if I did, he would pray for me. Thanks, Frank. It worked. Robert Kennedy, another strategic latency alum, reviewed the draft and provided important revisions. Don Gabrielson at SpaceX also provided invaluable editorial comments.

Feroz Khan at the Naval Postgraduate School shared his extraordinary expertise in South Asian security and provided comments on the border conflicts and the weapons employed by India, Pakistan and China. My South Asia Track 1.5 colleagues Drew Winner, Mike Lefever, Bob Swartz, Gillian Gayner, Dave Smith, Chris Clary, Anna Davari, Christine Craig, Linton Brooks, Yun Sun, Elisabeth Threlkeld, Sameer Lalwani, Dan Markey and Rich Mies shared their insights into the nature of modern conflict in South Asia. I hope my South Asian colleagues are amused and not insulted.

Vaughn Hudziak knows more about space technology than I ever will. Harry Flashman takes credit for everything; why stop now? Tom Bentley and Mitchell Reiss indulged me in thinking I could write a novel. Carol Winton was a fine cheerleader. My sons Max and Sam did

ACKNOWLEDGEMENTS

a good job pretending to be interested. The mistakes and indiscretions are mine alone.

CHAPTER ONE

Scorched Earth at the Top of the World

S hen Dingli sharpened his weapon on a flat stone he had found by the campfire. It was a metal spike that he had bound to a tree branch. The branch was straight and supple and would have made a decent short staff back at his kung fu training academy in Chengdu. But today, he was turning it into an improvised weapon for use against the Indian troops who were camped on the other side of the border, less than a kilometer away.

Colonel Shen had heard stories about hand-to-hand combat between Chinese and Indian soldiers in which sticks, spikes, spears, knives, rocks and all sorts of improvised weapons had been used by both sides. In one particularly brutal clash in 2020, dozens of soldiers from both sides were killed in a raucous brawl. For some reason, the commanders of both armies had instructed their troops not to use guns or artillery and to restrict their armament to medieval implements. His boss, the commander of the Western Theater Forces, gave him a direct order to make sure no shots were fired. So Dingli and his troops scavenged the surrounding Naku La mountainsides to find sticks and rocks and fashioned them into crude weapons like the ones he trained with growing up. His sifu, master Jang, had often said, "The best weapon is one that is available when you need it." He had practiced the short and long staff, chain whips, spear, axe, and various sword forms. He especially appreciated a Xing Yi form that used chopsticks as deadly weapons. This pole with a spike on it would do nicely in close-quarters combat unless somebody pulled a gun. He would be ready for that, too.

Why they were here in this remote outpost in the Himalayan mountains near Ladakh, he did not know. Col. Shen knew that there had been clashes here before and that the borders along the South Xinjiang Military District were not well marked so nobody really knew where the hell China stopped and India started. Another gift from the British colonial invaders, Dingli thought. The British had drawn the maps defining the borders of China, India, Tibet, Pakistan, Nepal, Bhutan, Afghanistan, and the perennially contested flashpoints throughout Jammu and Kashmir. Every Chinese student learned the history of such colonial insults in school. The Brits screwed up the borders by drawing the McMahon Line in 1914, which disregarded centuries of Chinese influence throughout the Karakoram region. Finally, president for life Xi would settle things once and for all. They were ready.

The British colonial occupiers sowed the seeds of this conflict in 1947 when they left South Asia with their tail between their legs as their empire crumbled after the Second World War, like they did in Afghanistan in the previous century, but not before dividing their former colonies into the new nations of India and Pakistan, again disrespecting China's ancient presence in the Ladakh region and setting the stage for decades of war and conflict over the contested borders of Kashmir, Assam, and Arunachal Pradesh. At least the 1962 War had put India on notice that China would not knuckle under to its delusions of Hindu supremacy. It was the same in Doklam in 2017, Dingli mused, when the Indians tried to stop us from building roads on our side of the border, and again in 2020 when we kicked their ass for constructing buildings on our side of the Line of Actual Control. Dingli assumed that this deployment was related to those earlier battles. But he didn't understand why the Western Theater Commander would limit them to fighting with medieval weapons. Why not put the Indians in their place, once and for all? We are strong now, and our Pakistani allies will help us stand up to these Indian bullies.

Lt. General Harinder Singh didn't see it that way. He had been here before, most recently in 2020 when his troops had "given those PLA ruffians a proper lashing," as he was fond of saying. Several of his best men had been bludgeoned to death in one particularly brutal melee. As commander of the Indian Army 14 Corp, Lt. General Singh had also received orders to make sure nobody under his command used their firearms. "The politicals want to make a point, but they don't have the stones for a real war. They don't understand us" his commanding officer, Major General Arun Menon, had explained wistfully. "War is not a game."

In 2016, then Col. Singh was deployed in Jammu and Kashmir when his troops crossed the Line of Control (LOC) to conduct a surgical strike against Jaish e Mohammed terrorists who had infiltrated from Pakistan and attacked an Indian Army convoy, killing a half dozen soldiers. He was back again in 2019 when another JeM attack killed almost 40 soldiers on the National Highway near Pulwama. Things had escalated rapidly, including the use of artillery and air power by India and Pakistan, resulting in significant casualties and an international crisis involving grandstanding pundits crowing on TV and social media about nuclear flashpoints in "the world's most dangerous battlefield."

The Americans claimed to have detected movements of nuclear weapons into firing positions, raising the specter of nuclear war. American spy satellites had tracked the deployment of India's nuclear-powered and nuclear-armed Arihant ballistic missile submarine, and Pakistani units armed with Hatf IX multiple rocket launchers carrying tactical nuclear weapons being transported to forward firing positions, as well as Pakistan's Agosta 90 B diesel-powered submarines armed with Babur 3 nuclear-tipped cruise missiles. A think tank wag joked on CNN that the fighting between nuclear-armed India and Pakistan in the Himalayas was "like two bald men fighting over a toupee." Pointless.

Singh supposed that was what the politicians were trying to avoid –

another pointless war. This time, the Chief of the Army Staff had told him directly: "Hold the line, but don't start World War Three." The Pakistani and PLA commanders gave the same orders. "Hold the line, but don't start World War Three."

The sun was setting over the Ladakh Range when Singh took his usual evening walk around the encampment. He had come to love these mountains despite the seemingly endless conflicts over the arbitrary borders that the British colonial powers had stupidly drawn before they were thrown out when India claimed its independence. That was something everyone agreed on, even the Americans, Chinese and Pakistanis. "All of us suffered at the hands of the British colonial armies. How did they do it?" he often mused. "How was it that so few Englishmen were able to expand their empire and dominate the world? You had to hand it to them. They were a hardy lot, the Brits. Guns, germs, and steel. We still speak their damn language. They did the same thing to the Middle East, and we're still paying for it."

As he walked and breathed the bright mountain air, Singh heard music coming from across the Galwan River from the PLA camp, less than a kilometer away. The Chinese soldiers were singing. Not bad, he thought. "Maybe I should get our boys to show them a thing or two about music. "He strode back to the barracks where his men were preparing for bed, called them to attention and addressed the group. "The enemy is assaulting our ears with noise from across the river. We shall blunt their auditory aggression with a rousing chorus. Assemble immediately in the training area, facing the river. No weapons."

The jawans gathered and began singing a favorite Hindi folk song as the afterglow of sunset faded and the stars awakened. They heard the Chinese singing and set to the task of countering it. The PLA troops sang louder, prompting the Indian soldiers to do the same. At first, it was comical, almost fun, as they yelled through the darkness at one another, moving toward the riverbank where both sides had engineering units building bridges in contested territory. The singing soon degenerated into crude insults: "Your father should have slept instead of fucking your mother," the jawans taunted. "Fuck your ancestors to the eighteenth generation," the Chinese soldiers shouted back. "Madarchods!" "Erbi!" Hundreds of young men lined the riverbank, hurling insults and making obscene gestures. Then, a rock hit an Indian soldier, and the battle was on. The troopers rushed at each other, splashing into the shallow river and streaming across the Bailey bridge that spanned the border. General Singh and Colonel Shen shouted at them to stop, with identical results. There was no going back.

Chinese and Indian troops hurled themselves at one another, kicking, spitting, gouging, and punching one another in an ugly orgy of violence. A Pandora's box full of suppressed emotions had unleashed a swarm of evil demons possessed with the will to kill and destroy their fellow humans. Harinder noticed several piles of men wrestling and writhing on the ground like packs of wild dogs, covered in dirt and blood, shredding one another with crude weapons. The young soldiers wielded sharpened sticks, some wrapped with barbed wire, machetes, clubs, bats, and slings to hurl rocks. Shen briefly admired the expert use by one of his soldiers of a spinning back fist that connected with an Indian soldier's jaw, knocking him senseless. A jawan hurled a rock onto the skull of a young PLA soldier, smashing it like a pumpkin. In anger, Shen expertly impaled the young jawan with his metal spike, killing him with a strike through the heart. The young Indian's eyes wide in disbelief as he breathed his last breath.

The shots came from the hills overlooking the impromptu battlefield as snipers began picking off random participants in the brawl unfolding below. Both Shen and Singh had prepositioned sharpshooters above the fray "just in case things got out of hand." Things were very much out of hand as Indian and Chinese snipers zeroed in on their unsuspecting prey, killing them with headshots that seemed to come from nowhere. Soon, the sky filled with small drones armed with explosives, a brutal tactic that both sides had learned from the Ukraine war. Shen and Singh had also both stationed drone operators in the hillside "just in case." The bomblets rained down on the melee as soldiers scattered in every direction, not knowing where the bullets and bombs were coming from or how to escape the tornado of death swirling around them.

Consistent with their similar age, training, military background, and current circumstances, Shen and Singh simultaneously ordered artillery strikes on the opposing camp, both thankful that they had dragged all that heavy equipment into the mountains with them. "Do we really need artillery for political theatre at the top of the world?" some commanders had questioned Singh. "We're not going to war, after all," they told him. "Just in case, we must have an armored brigade," Singh had argued. Singh knew well how to direct fires from the Bofors had proved decisive against the Pakistanis in Kashmir in 1999. He wasn't going to face off with the Chinese without them.

Indian Army gunners unleashed the full fury of their Bofors on Shen's forces while their PLA counterparts fired their PCL 181 Howitzers to strike the rear areas of the Indian encampment, killing scores of support and logistics personnel, including the road-building crews who were sent to consolidate anticipated territorial gains. "We need to be able to target the roads from the high ground," Shen had told his Western Command superiors. Now, the artillery was paying off, big time. Intelligence, surveillance, and reconnaissance (ISR) drones were providing both sides with precise targeting information for the gunners, who were now obliterating the makeshift encampments and demolishing key roads and resupply routes. With the rocks and body parts bouncing like popcorn from the barrage of mortar and cannon fire, the valley was returning to its prehistoric, pre-human state. Nobody would survive to claim victory.

At the same moment, both generals thought to themselves, "This looks bad. I better report that we have been attacked without warning or provocation and that we are defending ourselves and our position but need air support." Neither liked the idea of calling their commanding officers and telling them what was going on, but both knew that media reports would soon stir the pot with hyperbolic headlines about the fierce battle being fought at the top of the world and how brave soldiers were defending the honor of their respective nations. Then, the politicians would crank up the heat with demands for action to avenge Indian/Chinese aggression. Maybe air strikes would not guarantee victory, but they might at least muddy the waters sufficiently to obscure the reality, which was that they had bungled their way into a bloody disaster.

If the goal was to make it impossible to understand what the hell was happening on the battlefield, the air strikes achieved their objective. Indian Air Force Mig 29s from the 21 Air Wing at Leh bombed the valley battlefield, unable to provide close air support to Indian troopers because they were unable to distinguish between the Indian and Chinese units near the river or what was left of them. They did, however, cross the Line of Actual Control (LOAC) to strike the roads and PLA logistics supply areas north of the river, despite orders to stay on their side of the border and avoid engaging in air combat with Chinese fighters. "Make the point and come home. We don't want to start World War Three," were the orders from India's Western Command.

PLA Air Force jets had the same orders -- to bomb the valley but not engage Indian jets and not cross the border into Indian territory. Indian Migs and Chinese J-11s passed each other going opposite directions across the river, close enough to see the obscene gestures the pilots were making at one another as they crisscrossed the pathetic scene unfolding in the valley below. Both sides were limited by the altitude, which reduced their speed, maneuverability and the amount of fuel and munitions they could carry. The area near the river where the brawl started had become a hellish cauldron of senseless death, the rear areas behind them cut off on both sides by what was supposed to be symbolic artillery and air strikes, none of which were intended to set the stage for actual ground invasions of territory. The calculated political theater had become a grotesque bloodletting, and it was spiraling out of control.

CHAPTER TWO

The Gray Zone
Beyond the Battlefield

Indian web sites showed horrific pictures of mutilated bodies, and outraged television commentators howled for vengeance against the Chinese invaders. Chinese media at first dismissed the reports as American disinformation, then downplayed the conflict as a miscommunication, but were soon reporting that "a small group of saboteurs had crossed from India into Chinese territory to conduct terrorist attacks against Chinese researchers studying the effects of climate change on Himalayan communities." An official Communist Party spokeswoman reassured, "PLA border security units are currently dealing with the situation."

Behind closed doors, political leaders on both sides were apoplectic, demanding answers as to why military leaders had allowed the border situation to boil over. "This is the last thing in the world I need right now, and you morons go and start a fucking border war? We have elections fast approaching, and our poll numbers are not great. Now, the whole country is calling for me to stand up to China. I can't back down now!" Prime Minister Modi has survived multiple elections with his brand of Hindu nationalism and claims that he and India represent the underserved and under- represented people of the world. His BJP coalition also kept a close eye on food prices and keeping farmers happy throughout India's far-flung provinces. He vented to his trusted national security advisor, Ajit Doval, also known as India's James Bond. "I thought we told those idiots not to start World War Three!"

"Mr. Prime Minister, our military leaders are preparing a range of options. But, perhaps we should view this as an opportunity. With China already preoccupied on multiple fronts, domestic and foreign, and their economy already flagging, Beijing may not be in the mood for another conflict at this time. They've got their hands full with Washington breathing down their necks. Our intelligence people confirm that the Communist Party leadership is not happy with such unnecessary distractions, like border wars. Perhaps it is an opportunity to demonstrate to Chairman Xi the strength and confidence of the new India."

"What are you getting at?" Modi snapped. "Are you suggesting we escalate? Are you recommending we send reinforcements to the border?"

"No sir," Doval replied coolly. "Not more troops. We have developed a sophisticated array of hybrid warfare capabilities that would send Beijing a strong message but also leave them a way out. We could do to them what they are planning to do to the Americans, you know, give them a taste of their own medicine, as it were."

"Like what? More of your covert operations? Surgical strikes? Some sort of cyber-attack?"

"Sir, what if we sent them a thali plate, a sampler of our new capabilities, as a reminder that things have changed? You know what they say, never waste a good crisis."

"What would be included on this thali plate?"

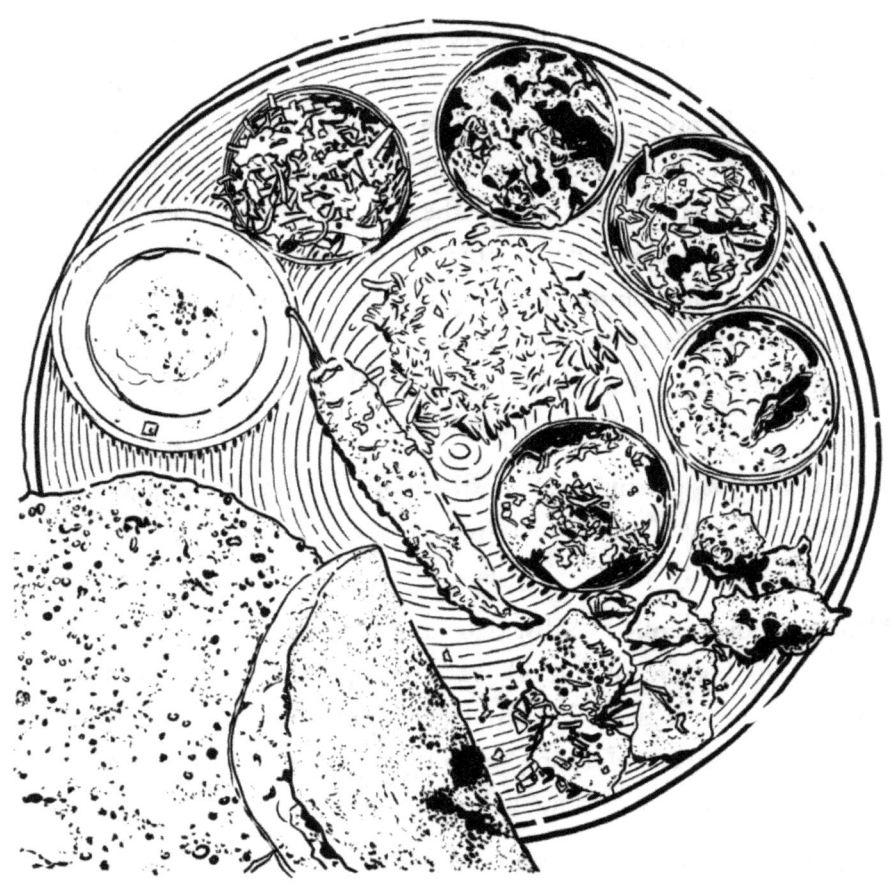

What would be on this thali plate?

"Well, I have in mind a full course meal, starting with an amuse bouche of cyber strikes on their critical infrastructure, followed by an entrée of interdiction of their vital shipping lines, topped off with a desert directed at their space assets. The entire feast would, of course, be completely unattributable and therefore deniable and designed to keep our pesky international friends from interfering with our little dinner party. Xi will get the message."

"What about Pakistan, Beijing's little friend? Will they stay on the sidelines? No, they'll unleash their terrorist brigades and pour gas on the fire."

"We should invite them to the party. In fact, let's serve them a special dish. I have something in mind, something they will not suspect. Something delicious."

In Beijing, Communist Party officials were indeed in disarray, as India's intelligence service, the Research and Analysis Wing (RAW), had reported. One group consisted of the "wolf warriors" who advocated sending reinforcements to the border, even if it meant escalating the crisis. "We can't let these Indian upstarts challenge our rightful claims in Aksai Chin, where our culture has been dominant for centuries. We must put them in their place. What will our adversaries think if we back down now? It would reek of weakness and a loss of face." urged Liu Shaye, a powerful foreign policy advisor. Others argued that retaking Taiwan should be the top military priority, not the obscure border regions.

President Xi remained impassive. He had consolidated his position as president for life years ago and restored the unquestioned power of the Communist Party, with him as its apex predator. Challenges to his power, both real and imagined, suffered swift and decisive punishment. His economic advisors saw the border war as a distraction from bigger issues, like the economy. "Now is not the time for this fight," argued Han Zheng, an influential economic advisor to President Xi. "We have other fish to fry. This border conflict gets us nothing." Xi remained stone-faced.

Watching the debate like hawks hovering over a field full of mice, PLA leaders carefully calculated who would win the argument before taking a position. Would the wolf warriors prevail and demand escalation, or would the economic pragmatists win the day? Most importantly, who would be blamed for turning the border into a massive shit show? General Jang, commander of the Western Theater, was prepared to pivot either way – send more troops to the border or bring them home. He had no dog in this fight either way. "If I was a betting man (as he was), Jang thought to himself, "I would put my money on the economic pragmatists. Xi is cautious by nature and not in a hurry to risk the $150 billion in trade between India and China, not to mention the sanctions that the United States and Europe would impose if they went to war with India. Why fight India, especially now? Pride?"

But Jang was wrong, and he lost that bet. Xi ended the meeting dispassionately and called Jang, selected members of the PLA, the Central Military Commission, and the Ministry of State Security (MSS), including intelligence chief Chen Wenwing, into a side office. Seated uncomfortably in a row of overstuffed green chairs along the red velvet curtains lining the room, Xi complemented Jang on outfoxing the Indian commanders and calling their bluff. "What were you singing that set them off?" Xi calmly asked Jang. "It was a folk song from Chengdu, written by Zhao Lei. It's popular among the soldiers, sir." Jang knew he was on thin ice. "The Indian soldiers on the other side of the river did not like your music, it seems," Xi said quietly. "I'm screwed," Jang thought. "Perhaps they were inspired to match our musical talent," Jang offered, hoping to lighten the mood, sweat stains now visible through the arm pits of his forest green PLA uniform. "It seems you are a very talented musician, General Jang. How do you suppose we will continue the concert? Do you have an encore?" "Sir, we have a tremendous orchestra. We can play any music the conductor wishes. What is your favorite?" "We will deliver the musical score to you shortly, General." "I'm a dead man," Jang thought.

Addressing the Communist Party officials in the room, President Xi appeared more animated as he laid out his instructions.

"We shall teach our Indian friends a lesson they will not soon forget. We will begin with a selection of cyber disruptions of their economy, as a reminder of their political weakness. Shut down their banking sector, including their ATMs. My friend prime minister Modi will get the message. Elections indeed! Let's see how not being able to get their money affects his polling numbers."

"Move six brigades to the border, raise the alert status of our strategic rocket forces, activate air defense units, and move naval forces close enough to the Straits of Malacca to get everyone agitated. Make sure that our actions attract plenty of attention. Use the hacker brigades to shape the environment on social media, especially Tic Tok and Instagram. Our symphony will crescendo with notes from our new instruments."

"And what about our Pakistani friends?" inquired Tang Zhao, a senior member of the Central Military Commission. "They will be eager to know their role in the orchestra."

"We shall invite our Pakistani friends to join the chorus by making as much noise as they can muster in Kashmir. They're good at making noise. It's what they do best, although they're pretty good at making nuclear weapons. And terrorists. The Indians will not be able to resist a little distraction along the Line of Control with Pakistan. Instruct the Pakistanis to demonstrate the firepower of the artillery we recently provided, the SH-15 howitzer, I believe it was."

"We also provided them with HQ-16 SAMs," interjected Tang Zhao. "Those could be quite effective against the Indian's Russian SU 30s. It's also an opportunity for Pakistan to show off the JF-17s and J-10s we supplied, and the new Yuan class submarines. It's not bad advertising, especially since the embarrassing performance of Russian hardware in Ukraine. Such a demonstration will boost sales."

"Thank you, Mr. Tang. Advertising indeed. At the appropriate time, invite the Pakistan Army to take a few of their tactical nuclear weapons out for a drive in the countryside. And perhaps some of their sea-based nuclear weapons as well. Direct our naval forces to make a port visit at Gwadar. Include a nuclear submarine. That will get the Americans' attention. Let us see how committed they are to helping their Indian ally. I doubt if they have the stomach for a real fight. And Chen, please have a little chat with General Jang. His singing is a bit off-key."

CHAPTER THREE

Escalation Without Off Ramps

As Chinese and Indian air, sea and land forces began the gruesome choreography of closing the distance between them, an electrical storm of cyber strikes rippled across both countries. Years of preparation to infiltrate the control systems of civil infrastructure made it relatively simple for cyber teams in Delhi and Beijing to simultaneously unleash chaos in the water treatment, transportation management, energy production, and especially financial systems across India and China. Having pushed the buttons to activate pre-placed malicious software that had been implanted for just such an occasion, billions of Chinese and Indian citizens, almost half of the world's population, reacted in what could have been predictable ways.

an electrical storm of cyberstrikes rippled across both countries

Power outages, water shortages, chaotic traffic, business closures, cancellations, delays, and shuttered banks were so common in both countries that people viewed them more with resigned exasperation than political outrage. No power? Nothing new. Planes can't fly? Maybe tomorrow. Snarled traffic? Same as always. Can't get money from the ATM? Everything will just have to wait. Having climbed out of poverty and into the conveniences afforded by technology within their lifetimes, most Indian and Chinese citizens were resilient – and fatalistic. "What can I do?" was a common refrain across half of humanity, accompanied by a resigned shrug. The cyber war was a pain in the ass but not the strategic weapon that advocates had claimed and didn't translate into the hoped-for political upheaval that was supposed to put pressure on political leaders.

Moving troops to the border and ships into strategic positions, however, got the world's attention. Intelligence services across the globe informed their governments that there was a major war brewing in South Asia. All of the classic warning signs flashed blood red. HUMINT, SIGINT and GEOINT left no doubt about what was happening. India and China were going to war.

In response, governments expressed concern and called for restraint. The global media, however, was anything but restrained, blasting hyperbolic headlines about "Nuclear Storm Clouds on the World's Highest Battlefield." "On the Brink!" screamed The Hindu. "Chinese Warships Threaten Vital Shipping Lanes," warned the Indian Express. "India Crosses the Line," charged the People's Daily. "Not One Inch!" cried the South China Morning Post. The Bulletin of the Atomic Scientists moved the doomsday clock a minute closer to midnight. Television commentators whipped the flames, some calling for action to avenge historic insults, others blaring about nuclear Armageddon. Demonstrators burned flags and demanded retribution for their murdered heroes, just as Modi and Xi had feared. Social media cranked up the heat with wild stories and AI-generated fake videos, including one of Modi appearing to mock Xi. "It looks like Winnie the Pooh got his paw stuck in the honey jar, and he may get it lopped off," taunted an Indian deep fake video made to look like Modi was mocking Xi's resemblance to Winnie the Pooh, referring to a meme that had been banned in China.

Chinese hackers responded with deep fakes of Xi demeaning Modi as nothing more than a "pathetic Eeyore," Winnie the Pooh's downtrodden donkey sidekick. Pro-China cartoonists depicted Xi as a muscular Pooh bear with slashing claws and gnashing teeth, shredding Indian troops against a Himalayan Mountain background. Indian satirists showed a pleading Xi sinking in quicksand surrounded by world leaders, smiling blithely with their arms crossed, happy to see him crying for help as he disappeared into a steaming bog. A series of deep fake videos depicted Xi and Modi in a variety of obscene sexual positions. Worse yet, deep fakes appeared to show both leaders threatening nuclear war. Unconfirmed photos of warships, military convoys, drone strikes, human rights abuses, and nuclear explosions flooded the airwaves and were instantly magnified by the Internet. Foreign journalists were barred from the border regions, and their press corps was placed under emergency controls. Nobody could discern what was really happening.

Disinformation campaigns designed to shape and control perceptions caused further confusion and accelerated the pace of events. India's intelligence service, the Research and Analysis Wing (RAW), cultivated an onslaught of false reporting that they planted on African internet sites, which soon spread throughout the world. Fox News took the bait and recycled a bogus report that Chinese troops were eating their prisoners. China's Ministry of State Security planted stories about India rounding up Christians and Muslims and putting them in concentration camps, sparking outrage in America and throughout the

Middle East. Volunteer hacker groups stoked the flames with horror stories of rape, torture, and corruption, some of it true.

For decades, the US had been the honest broker who intervened in South Asia's conflicts to cool things down. Both sides had welcomed American diplomacy to deescalate their history of recurring crises. But things had changed in recent years, and nobody wanted American firefighters to douse the flames. Saudi Arabia, Turkey, and Brazil stepped into the diplomatic vacuum with offers to mediate, but nobody took them seriously. Moscow offered to negotiate a truce, but Modi and Xi scoffed at Putin's offer. That was the last thing anyone needed. The United Nations passed a resolution calling on both parties "to exercise all possible mechanisms of peace and security dialog to ensure the maintenance of established norms of peaceful coexistence," whatever that means. It didn't help. The fuse was lit and burning fast.

As the march of folly stumbled towards war, analysts likened the situation to the onset of the First World War, in which Europe's feckless leaders bumbled their way into a catastrophe that nobody wanted or believed possible. Surely, India and China would pull back from the brink. But like The Great War that had enflamed Europe in 1911, massive mobilization took on a life of its own and became seemingly unstoppable. And like German Field Marshall Alfred von Schlieffen, who devised the blitzkrieg plan to overwhelm French defenses quickly, Indian and Chinese military leaders accepted the twisted logic that "mobilization means war." Once started, any delay in preparing to fight would give the enemy an advantage.

And since multi-domain warfare meant that air, sea, land, cyber, space and strategic nuclear systems were supposed to be coordinated and interconnected, everything had to move in concert, like an opera production. Ships, aircraft, land forces, defenses, and cyber and space systems were all part of the military "Internet of Things." Massive amounts of data flowing from millions of sensors – on ships, planes, drones, people, equipment, supplies, from every inch of every battlefield: sea, air, land, cyber, and space – all churning out megabits of inchoate information that was supposed to help battlefield commanders and national decision-makers win the war.

When collected, combined, and analyzed, all the information coming in from all those sensors was supposed to provide tactical and strategic advantages. Artificial intelligence algorithms help collect, sort and bundle information about the "operational environment." That tangle of information is supposed to enable commanders to identify enemy locations, numbers and vulnerabilities and concentrate their advantages to exploit opportunities with speed and precision. Joint, all-domain command and control (JADC2) is supposed to "get inside the enemy's OODA loop," a popular military acronym for Observe, Orient, Decide, Act. According to the theory, the commander who gets the best information fastest has the advantage. Indian and Chinese commanders were deep into the process of getting swamped with information, which was flowing to them via land, sea, air and space-based communication systems. AI was supposed to make sense of all that data. Whoever figured out the puzzle first would have the upper hand, at least in theory.

The problem, in this case, was that neither side really wanted to go to war. And neither side could make sense of the tsunami of multi-domain data that was overwhelming them. The whole thing was a colossal fuck-up from the beginning, bad political theatre, a sick joke. But now things were moving fast. All the exquisite capabilities they had been buying and building were doing what they were supposed to do and doing it quickly, with little time for careful consideration. The dogs of war were unleashed accidentally.

In Beijing, Xi inquired about the execution of his orders. "Mr. President," Tang Zhou reported:

"Our forces are massing toward the border, as ordered. The strategic rocket forces are on alert, air defenses as well, the air force is deploying jets and missiles to the Western Theatre, and our navy is moving toward the Straits, including a Jin class nuclear submarine. I think the Indians will get the message."

"And what has become of our cyber gifts?"

"Sir, we are still calculating the damage, but it appears that the Indians were largely unaffected. They seem to have shrugged them off. I'm sorry, sir."

"Shrugged them off?"

"Yes, sir. The cyber intrusions on their infrastructure appear to have achieved their physical objectives but did not produce the hoped-for political reactions. Indians, it seems, are accustomed to such inconveniences as blackouts and blockages."

"I see."

In Delhi, national security advisor Doval updated Modi.

"Mr. Prime Minister, the army is moving infantry and light armor brigades to the Line of Actual Control, the air force has established forward bases for close air support, our navy is in position to declare a Maritime Exclusion Zone (MEZ), the strategic forces are on high alert, and the Arihant SSBN is en route to the Andaman Islands. I think the Chinese will get the message. The Pakistan Army wouldn't dare deploy their nukes. This isn't their fight."

"Are the Chinese people enjoying the cyber treats we delivered? They must be frustrated and blaming President Xi and the CCP for the collapse of their infrastructure."

"Sir, our cyberattacks were executed as planned and struck their targets. However, their systems seem to have rebounded rather quickly."

"Aren't the Chinese people blaming Xi for the chaos? What about their economy?"

"Sir, the Chinese people appear to be rallying behind their president, blaming us for their hardships."

"I see. But will they continue to stick with him if confronted with the prospect of even greater sacrifices, such as a stinging defeat in the mountains, a cutoff of their oil, and the crushing of their little Pakistani friends?

"Sir, they appear to be matching our escalatory actions, including sending reinforcements to the border and moving nuclear assets. A Jin-class SSBN is moving in the direction of the Straits. And they appear to be moving SS 21s to launch sites on the Tibetan plateau. The Pakistanis are escalating in Kashmir and appear to be moving tactical nuclear weapons to forward firing positions. The Nasr battlefield nuclear rockets are on the move. I'm sure it's all for show, but..."

"Are they not getting the message? Do we need to make a stronger demonstration of our resolve? This is the new India. We will not be intimidated by a tin-pot Chinese dictator, their Pakistani lap dogs, or anyone else, including the self-righteous Americans! Those days are over. How about a test launch of Agni 5 to show we can reach out and touch Beijing? Or a nuclear test? We need to do more of those anyway. The scientists are always bugging me about it. Are we positioned to impose a Maritime Exclusion Zone? Let's see how they like having their oil supply cut off."

"Sir, with so many things already in play, perhaps it would be wise to allow the situation to germinate for a bit. See what happens; give them a chance to back down. Our diplomats could reach out. We could talk to Moscow.

"Didn't we set up a hotline a few years ago?"

"Yes, but nobody uses it. They don't even answer the phone. To be honest, either we or Pakistan. It's a joke, sir."

"I want a nuclear test. A big one to send a message like the Russians did to Kennedy with the tsar bomb in 1961. The world needs to understand the new India. The scientists have been lobbying for a test for years. Let's show Beijing how things have changed."

"Yes, sir. Just a single test or a series of detonations? The scientists have a long list of things they want to try – tactical weapons, strategic, a hydrogen bomb. The test site is ready. How strong of a message do you want to send?"

"I want to show the world that India has arrived on the main stage, that Hindustan is defining the new world order. Our time has come. We're tired of waiting."

"And what of the Pakistanis? They are sure to follow our lead, as they did when we tested in 1998. Do we care if they test, too? China is bound to follow with tests of its own. And the Iranians. And the North Koreans. Maybe others. The Americans will go crazy about breaking the moratorium on nuclear testing, the test ban treaty, and their beloved Nonproliferation Treaty. There are sure to be sanctions."

"Unhen chodo. To hell with the NPT. I'm sick of the Americans making all the rules. No more nuclear apartheid. Nuclear deterrence is working fine for us, the same as it did for them in the Cold War. Sanctions hurt them more than us anyway. Let them all test their nuclear weapons. It's just a demonstration. We're not actually using them, for god's sake. Give the order. Tell the scientists to test whatever they want."

"Yes, sir. I'll give you the order. And the timing?"

"Immediately. As soon as possible. I want to make a statement. I'm not backing down. We're not going to back down."

Five days later, in the Thar desert, Indian scientists announced that they had conducted a series of five underground detonations. Like the tests in May of 1998, there was confusion about the actual results. India claimed to have achieved yields from 1 to 500 kilotons, first supposedly a tactical weapon and the latter a thermonuclear or hydrogen bomb. The confusion was exacerbated by the premature release of an official statement asserting success several hours before the completion of the actual tests and the inability of the global detection system operated by the Comprehensive Test Ban Treaty Organization (CTBTO) to verify all five claimed detonations also liked in 1998. A 500-kiloton test should have been easily detected if it had occurred. But the political message was clear: India was escalating the crisis.

Pakistan responded immediately with five tests of their own, all verified by the CTBTO in yields from 1 to 50 kilotons, described by Islamabad as reinforcing their "full spectrum deterrence strategy." China was next with four detonations at its Lop Nur test site, followed by North Korea, which claimed to have demonstrated its capability to reach the American homeland with thermonuclear weapons. Global monitors detected novel radiation signatures and x-rays from Russia's arctic test site at Novaya Zemla, which Moscow declared was "an entirely new type of weapon for which the West has no defense."

Iran issued a statement that it "can test a nuclear weapon but has decided not to do so at this time." The United States condemned the outburst of nuclear testing and called for the immediate restoration of the moratorium on nuclear detonations. Russia and China blocked a UN resolution condemning the tests, joined by India, Pakistan, Iran and North Korea. Anti-nuclear protesters called on the US to unilaterally disarm as a good-faith effort to reduce global nuclear dangers. The Bulletin of the Atomic Scientists moved its doomsday clock to 30 seconds to midnight, the closest ever.

The orgy of nuclear bravado, however, was only the middle act in the unfolding political drama. President Xi reconvened his inner circle to lay out his next move.

"Our Indian neighbors want to demonstrate their Hindu machismo by playing nuclear games. We shall indulge them with some theater of our own. Some of you are aware of certain capabilities that we have been developing for such circumstances. These include a variety of space assets that provide us with a range of options. You may have heard about the wargame conducted at Lawrence Livermore Laboratory, in which the Americans acted quickly to seize the high ground. A well-placed intelligence asset reported the details. We must take the high ground. For now, we shall use our anti-satellite weapons to neutralize some of India's military space assets. Let's see how they like being deaf, dumb, and blind."

"Sir, shall we utilize a laser strike or a kinetic strike? How much drama do you want to provoke? A strike from our ground station or our space assets? A kinetic strike will create broader consequences due to the debris. The Americans will react. A laser strike from the ground or our satellites would contain the damage and thus would have the advantage of being deniable and keep the Americans out of our business."

"I think a bit of both should make our point to India and to the others who are not yet persuaded of our technical accomplishments or our will to act. We have some other cards to play, as some of you already know. The Indians and their American friends are about to understand the full meaning of the parable about the nine blind men of Hindustan."

"Am I correct to assume that you would like to keep Blossom Flower in your back pocket?"

"Yes, it's good to have a flower in your pocket."

China's investments in military technology were paying big dividends, especially in the space domain, where America and its allies were most vulnerable. Despite a defense budget that dwarfed that of China and forces far in excess of any other nation's military, the Americans remained shockingly unprepared to meet the challenge of multi-domain warfare. Despite years of warnings from Congressional hearings, think tanks, academic books, articles, studies, and high-level commissions urging the Pentagon to address the China challenge, America was still preparing to fight the last wars. Most surprising was the military's reliance on highly vulnerable space navigation and communications, including commercial satellites, for essential functions of US military operations. As the Chinese fully understood, no other nation was so dependent on space or better positioned to do something about its dangerous exposure. But it didn't.

Knowledgeable insiders wrote fictional accounts to warn about a future US-China conflict (and India's role in it), such as Peter Singer and August Cole's Ghost Fleet and Admiral James Stavridis and Eliot Ackerman's 2034. US Space Command, NRO, and the Space Development Agency were aware of the problem but couldn't find a way to escape their dependency on the established network of commercial contractors, whose government contracts were often a small part of their global business model. The US government was just one among many clients. The Pentagon knew it needed the private sector to compete and win in space but couldn't figure out how to convince its contractors to put US national security over profitability or their personal political views. Nobody wanted to see a repeat of Elon Musk's interference with Ukraine's Starlink access because he wanted to protect Russian forces from Ukrainian drone strikes. What if every big company and every billionaire had their own foreign policy?

A few entrepreneurs, like Lucky Slater, questioned the business model that put the US military at the mercy of a few big commercial venders, especially if they depended on global supply chains for critical materials. Why not replace them with a dynamic network of fast-moving American innovators? The Pentagon was aware of the problems bogging down its archaic procurement system and had established a few experimental sand boxes, like the Defense Innovation Unit (DIU) in Silicon Valley, AFWERX for the Air Force, NAVALX for the Navy, Army Futures Command, and SOFWERX for the Special Operations Command to meet the near-term technology needs of the warfighters. But they still couldn't build big systems like aircraft carriers, inter-continental ballistic missiles, submarines or fighter jets. Lucky argued that small companies like his could meet the demand for space technology. For better and for worse, military and commercial interests in space were deeply entwined, like creeping vines on an old tree. SPACECOM would have to protect the whole network of publicly and privately owned satellites that were integrated throughout the national security space infrastructure. But it didn't.

entwined, like creeping vines on an old tree

SPACECOM had started discussions with its key contractors, but only a few corporate leaders had security clearances. The people running innovative start-ups didn't have clearances, and most of the entrepreneurs didn't want them. Government officials wanted to warn them about the mounting threats from China and Russia but couldn't because the information about Chinese and Russian offensive capabilities in space was so highly classified and would reveal sensitive sources and methods. US officials wanted to warn about a growing array of exotic weapons being developed and deployed from ground stations and space-based platforms, like the directed energy beams and high-power microwaves that were already probing and disrupting American satellites. They wanted to tell the commercial companies

28

about the kinetic anti-satellite weapons and the specialized nuclear weapons being deployed in space by Russia and China. They wanted to tell them about the tractor beams that sounded like science fiction and the secret moon base that China and Russia were building. They wanted to warn them about the cyber infiltration of their satellites that had already compromised so many American secrets. But they didn't.

What they could share was the analysis coming from the Space Situational Awareness experts, like Carissa Moore's group at Livermore Lab. They could describe what would happen if somebody shot down a satellite and created a bunch of space debris that collided with other satellites and snowballed into an avalanche of space junk. How it got started wasn't important. The point was that their investments were at risk of being demolished. They needed to get their commercial partners to start working on ways to defend their satellites and ground stations and to help clean up the mess if space got dangerously polluted with space junk. They needed to develop a Plan B if the whole GPS got knocked out. If space war was coming, it was time to prepare. But they didn't.

directed energy beams and high-power microwaves

CHAPTER FOUR

Crowded, Contested and Chaotic

"Someday soon, a piece of space junk is going to collide with a satellite and turn it into a rain of death for everything else in low Earth orbit (LEO). There are already over 30,000 pieces of space debris bigger than a baseball floating around out there, and any one of them could be the kiss of death for our entire space architecture."

For most of the people in the room, these words from Colonel Yater were simply stating the obvious. That was the whole reason for the wargame. Of course, nothing is "floating" out there; everything in orbit is going 17,500 miles per hour. "That's one hell of a fastball," Carissa thought to herself. "There's a lot more than just baseball-sized junk threatening our satellites. Yater doesn't know what he's talking about."

There are over a million pieces of space junk if you count the flecks of paint and chunks of old satellites, including the mess made by the Chinese anti-satellite weapon test (ASAT) in 2007 and the lesser fallout caused by India's ASAT test in 2019. Dr. Carissa Moore had come up with the idea to host a wargame to show what would happen if that space junk were weaponized. As a scientist at Lawrence Livermore National Laboratory (LLNL), she managed the Space Situational Awareness (SSA) program that tracks space debris and models its trajectories to predict dangers to satellites. What would happen if a collision created a thermo-spherical wall of death, like a shotgun blast ripping through LEO? She already knew the answer, but hopefully, the wargame would show everyone how bad things could get.

Dr. Moore had invited all the big players in the space game. Col. Yater commanded the US Space Command's (SPACECOM) Space Delta 2, the group in charge of Space Domain Awareness. They worked together with her group to track things in space and issue warnings about potential threats. SPACECOM satellites and tracking stations around the world monitor the orbital circus of satellites, and Carissa's team used the data they collected to issue warnings about impending collisions. SPACECOM's recruitment and retention benefitted from the fact that many of its tracking stations were located at world-class surfing and skiing locations, including Vandenberg, Maui, Half Moon Bay, Australia and near the slopes in Colorado, close to SPACECOM headquarters. SPACECOM units like the 18th and 15th Space Surveillance Squadrons attracted more than their fair share of big wave surfers and high-flying skiers.

Carissa liked working with guys like Major Jeff Clark, who ran the tracking station at Half Moon Bay, next to Mavericks, and his friend, Major Lance Hamilton, who had declined promotion to stay in Maui, near Jaws, the monster wave at Peahi. The same was true for Major Burton in Colorado, who retired from the military and continued his role as a civilian contractor to keep skiing in the Rockies. She liked working with them but sometimes wondered if they were more committed to the waves and the snow than the mission. She would never allow that on her team. Dr. Moore demanded one hundred percent commitment. She was relieved that they had committed to attend the wargame.

Also attending the wargame were representatives from all the big US Government (USG) space operators: SPACECOM, Space Systems Command, Strategic Command (STRATCOM), NASA, Air Force, National Geospatial Agency (NGA), CIA and the big brains from the national laboratories – Jet Propulsion Lab (JPL), Air Force Research Lab (AFRL), Naval Research Lab (NRL), Johns Hopkins Advanced

Physics Lab (APL) and of course, Sandia and Los Alamos labs. Carissa had also invited her mentor from the National Reconnaissance Office (NRO), George Downing, who gave her the idea to convene the wargame in the first place. The National Intelligence Officer (NIO) for Space, Lisa Owens, and Stephanie Gilmore from the White House National Security Council (NSC) were attending as well.

At George's insistence, Carissa had invited representatives from commercial space companies –the big contractors like Boeing and Lockheed Martin, the launch companies like Orbital, United Launch Services, and SpaceX, imagery providers such as Maxar and Planet, along with start-ups like Relativity, Astra, and Slingshot, who were making small satellites, 3D printing rockets, and using artificial intelligence (AI) and machine learning (ML) to collect and monetize satellite information. She had even invited the controversial owner of a global media conglomerate that depended on satellites to broadcast music and entertainment. The point of the wargame was to bring the government space community together with the commercial space companies to explore what would happen if all hell broke loose and we lost our eyes and ears in space. How bad would it be if a disaster wiped out the satellites?

Nobody can hear you scream in space, but there's plenty of noise when you get a bunch of space experts get together. Space is a tight-knit community on *Earth*, and people mostly know each other. That's partly because when people retire from the government they take jobs with the private sector, either with the big contractors or the start-ups. Rumor had it that Col. Yater was angling for a job with the freewheeling entrepreneurs at SpaceX. Dr. Moore hoped the game would show everyone how depended they were on space and that the entire network of interconnected space systems was in danger of collapse. She had also invited her friend Lucky Slater, a controversial free spirit, rule-breaker, and tech entrepreneur whose company was 3D printing rockets and satellites. What set Lucky apart was that he only sold his products to the US and allied countries and vowed never to help China's space program. "This is a competition, not a love festival," he liked to say. "There are winners and losers in this game. You don't get participation trophies in geopolitics."

Carissa knew quite a bit about baseball. Her dad had been the clubhouse and equipment manager for the Baltimore Orioles, and she had grown up roaming Camden Yards stadium. When it opened in 1992, it was the envy of the major leagues – a modern, retro-cool downtown mecca for America's favorite pastime. She loved the Orioles and became even more devoted to them after her dad died of cancer. He played catch with her, taught her how to hit, and even introduced her to Hall of Famer Frank Robinson when she was ten. Carissa had a picture of the three of them mounted in her office.

Her mom, Fannie Moore, was a high-school science teacher in Baltimore, known for her fierce advocacy of STEM training for inner-city kids. After two years at Towson State, and with the urging of a math professor who had recognized her aptitude for STEM, Carissa transferred to the University of Maryland to study physics. Her brain just worked that way. She turned down the Air Force Academy, which had urged her to follow in the footsteps of Dr. Mae Jemison, the first black female astronaut. She wanted to do research, not fly jets and wear a uniform. She was a science nerd and proud of it.

After getting her Ph.D. in astrophysics at the University of Rochester, Carissa had a fellowship at Johns Hopkins University, Applied Physics Lab, partly to stay close to her mom and partly to pursue her research on electromagnetic effects in the upper atmosphere and beyond. That's where she published her controversial view that certain kinds of electromagnetic pulses could propagate through the thermosphere, past the accepted starting point for space, through LEO and MEO and into the exosphere. The paper was based on data from a NASA-sponsored sensor package that she had helped design and place on the International Space Station. The paper was published in a respected physics journal, and she won the prestigious Hans Bethe prize and medal for her research.

If true, Dr. Moore's theory posed two big problems. The first was scientific. Suppose ninety-nine percent of the atmosphere ended at the Karman Line, roughly 60-70 miles above Earth. What were the properties of the one percent of gases extending outward through the thermosphere and beyond? Dr. Moore maintained that even sparse gases could have big consequences for electromagnetic propagation, especially lasers. What she did not appreciate at the time were the implications of her work for electromagnetic warfare. She questioned the standard "layers of the atmosphere" model in which the troposphere, stratosphere, mesosphere, thermosphere, and exosphere were layered on top of one another, easily distinguishable. Carissa argued that this was as simplistic and outdated as thinking of electrons as little spheres orbiting a nucleus. Dr. Moore favored a more nuanced, blended view of the space domain through which physical phenomena could traverse, aided by very thin concentrations of gases that facilitated energy transfer. She insisted that "it's all connected" and that particles flow through the layers "like little rivers in space."

like little rivers in space

Her research attracted the attention of Lawrence Livermore National Lab, where she joined the space research team that she now directs.

The second problem caused by her theory was bureaucratic. If, as she argued, space technically started in the mesosphere, before the Karman Line, the official government demarcations between agency responsibilities would be scrambled like Yahtzee dice. The Air Force was responsible for defending the troposphere, where planes fly, and the stratosphere, where high-altitude balloons and a few specialized aircraft fly. The Space Force takes over responsibility in the thermosphere, where most satellites operate in low Earth orbit (LEO), including those belonging to the multitude of government agencies that operate military and scientific satellites. Carissa's view challenged the conventional lines of demarcation and the divisions of responsibility based on them. If space started closer to Earth, and electromagnetic effects traversed freely through the traditional zones of responsibility, who would be the lead agency responsible for electromagnetic warfare? What about kinetic effects in space and hypersonic weapons? What about high-altitude spy balloons?

Like the territorial divisions between the regional military commands that divide up the globe *(CENTCOM and INDOPACOM in South Asia, and EUCOM, AFRICOM and CENTCOM over the Middle East)*, Carissa's research set off territorial alarm bells for SPACECOM, the Air Force, and all the agencies whose missions depend on space. Strategic Command's *(STRATCOM)* nuclear command and control system is entirely space-dependent. The Army, Navy, Air Force, Marines and Coast Guard all depend on satellite communications *(SATCOM)* and global positioning satellites *(GPS)* for essential operations such as navigation, intelligence, surveillance, and reconnaissance *(ISR)*, the eyes and ears of all military operations.

The Missile Defense Agency (MDA) is supposed to track and shoot down enemy missiles in space. The National Geospatial Agency (NGA), the super-secret National Reconnaissance Office (NRO), and the National Security Agency (NSA) are all mission-focused on space. Even CYBERCOM, the military command responsible for cyber defense and offense, claims space as its area of responsibility (AOR) because space assets are key targets of cyberattacks. Plus, the budget implications were astronomical – a point very much on the radar of several Congressional committees, and the White House. Who owns space? Carissa's wargame was guaranteed to poke that hornet's nest.

The problem that her mentor George had expressed to Carissa was that the private sector doesn't give a damn about how the US Government divides up space. They had discussed it while she was at Johns Hopkins, where they met while she was a researcher on a project sponsored by George's super-secret agency, the NRO. "We have lots of plans for how to conduct a war in space," he liked to say, "but no plans for what happens in space during a war." Who owns space? Nobody. Private companies have been shooting satellites into orbit for decades, with hardly any government controls. George was obsessed with how our whole society has gradually become totally dependent on commercial space for everything from business and transportation to entertainment, food, and energy. "The global economy would collapse if we lost the satellites." He warned. "It's not just war and peace that depends on space, but the tools we depend on for everyday life. Everything is entangled in a swirling mesh of space robots. "

"We think we are in control," George warned, "but we're not. Those private companies could care less about what the dweebs in the government think." The billionaire space jockeys were lofting constellations of thousands of satellites into orbit. Smaller companies had cracked the code of how to launch satellites, enabling scores of small companies to fling objects into LEO, MEO and even further out into GEO. They didn't need help or permission from anyone. Lucky Slater, for example, had founded a company to build and orbit a private space station equipped with 3D printing machines to manufacture a variety of products in space.

Slater was a renegade entrepreneur, a space cowboy known for his lurid Hawaiian shirts, long hair, shorts and flip-flops, which he wore to corporate meetings. Slater adhered to a strict "act first, ask permission later" philosophy. Nobody seemed to know what he was up to. Quirky, ruthless, and brilliant, he bragged that he would be the first person to visit his Malibu space station. He planned to live in space someday. Slater was fiercely patriotic and vowed never to sell his technology to America's adversaries. Other companies were perfectly happy to sell their wares to the highest bidder, which was usually China. Some fell into the trap of raising cash from mysterious, deep-pocket investors, only to have their intellectual property stolen from under their noses by hidden Chinese partners. After years of lobbying to remove export controls, many US technology companies were assisting foreign space programs, despite FBI warnings that they were supporting the secret space programs of America's adversaries. Globalization raises all boats, including the bad guys'.

Part of the problem for the US government and the commercial sector is that so much information about space missions and technologies is highly classified, and nobody can talk about the issues facing the community. Even inside the government, space programs are so compartmented that officials struggle to know what they are allowed to talk about and what they can share with private companies, even the ones they partner with. Only a very small cadre has all the clearances needed to see the big picture. George was one of those people. That's why he was worried.

Carissa had resisted getting her top-secret clearance but ultimately gave in to George's pleas. "Carissa, we need you." She didn't want to be grilled about smoking the occasional blunt or explain her grad school fling with a brilliant young Russian physicist, Andrei Wasilewski. She had run into him recently at a physics conference, and they had stirred the coals a bit. Andrei was tall and gaunt, with ice-blue eyes and a shock of close-cropped white-blond hair. He seemed to hear the music of the spheres, but she suspected that he was a bit on the spectrum. "Am I supposed to report every sexual encounter to our security office?" she wondered. "It was just one night." But she knew the answer. She kept putting off reporting it, anticipating the insinuating questions that the pug-faced counterintelligence officer would ask about their pillow talk. "Did you and Andrei discuss your work?" Of course, they had discussed scientific concepts. They were attending a scientific conference. Do they think the US government controls science? She hated the bureaucracy of the clearance process, the endless forms and the stupid questions. Everyone hates it, but they tolerate it because the work is important. "Now George wants me to take the damn polygraph so he can read me into some more stuff that I don't want to know about.

Andrei is a scientist, not a spy. He's too weird to be a spy." Everybody hates the clearance process, especially the polygraph.

Dozens of countries were joining the space race by launching their satellites or paying others to do it for them. The final frontier was looking more like the wild west. "Space looks like the start line of the Boston marathon -- or driving in India." George quipped in his thick Boston accent. He had run in the Boston marathon and traveled to New Delhi as part of a US government initiative to share space technologies with India. He got sick with Delhi belly on the road to visit the Taj Mahal and vowed never to go back, forever associating the commotion of India's roads and its most famous tourist attraction with explosive diarrhea. He regretted making the analogy. India was fast becoming a leading space power, and he might have to go back there some day.

Joining the rapidly expanding list of space-faring nations, developing nations such as Vietnam, Pakistan, and Ethiopia were now operating their satellites. The declining cost of space launch services made it possible for almost anyone to put something into orbit. Even North Korea successfully launched a Sputnik-like satellite into LEO, although all it did was broadcast the speeches of Kim Jong Un and his dynastic predecessors. Countries and companies throughout the world promoted their space bling as symbols of national and corporate pride. Elon Musk launched a cherry-red Tesla with a dummy driver into orbit. Every day more countries and companies were putting more things into orbit. Carissa and George had designed the wargame to highlight the threats posed by the increasingly crowded, contested, and chaotic space environment.

CHAPTER FIVE

Carissa's Wargame

On the day of the wargame, Carissa divided the attendees into four teams: blue, white, green and red. Blue was the USG team, populated by Carissa's SPACECOM buddies and government agency representatives. White was the private sector, consisting of Lucky Slater and a group of entrepreneurs and government contractors. The green team played the role of a generic US ally, such as Japan, Australia, or Israel. The green team was populated with regional experts in Asia, Europe, and the Middle East. The red team had the fun job of channeling adversary intentions, played by a group of experts on Russia and China. Carissa, George, and members of Carissa's Livermore staff would serve as the control group, aided by LLNL interns.

The scenario involved a border war that escalated to become a full-scale war, including the possible use of nuclear weapons. All four teams were given a supply of air, sea, ground, space, and cyber assets to cope with the scenario as it unfolded, guided by the control team. The goal was to see how space assets fared in a modern global war.

The instructions to the teams were to advance their interests in the conflict while protecting their space assets. Other than that, there were no rules. "All's fair in love and war," Carissa said sardonically to the teams after explaining the scenario and sending them to their separate game rooms to plot their next moves. The interns assigned to each group helped the teams report their moves to the control group, which would evaluate the moves and report back on the evolving state of play.

The wargame achieved its objective. The border war escalated rapidly to include the use of conventional, nuclear, cyber, and space weapons. The control group tried to slow down the march to war by offering diplomatic off-ramps, but the teams pushed the scenario to exploit every inch of advantage. "Why not? What do we have to lose?" said a green team participant." It's just a game; there's no cost for taking risks." others agreed. "We're here to disrupt the status quo." said another. "Do you want to win or just survive?"

As expected, deterrence failed. The red team employed all the weapons at their disposal early in the conflict to put the blue team on the defensive. "The best defense is a good offense," the red players reasoned. Echoing Russian, Chinese and North Korean thinking, the red team players agreed, "If we hit them hard enough, they'll see that it's not in their interests to keep going." One red team player asked, "What if blue intervenes to help green like they said they would?" "They won't if we hit them hard enough," the group decided. "Go big or go home!" they joked as they sent their decision to attack to the control group. Red had concluded that it was not in Blue's interest to risk its security to save Green.

The intern assigned to the red team, Eileen Gu, sent her game notes to the control group. She was in the first year of a graduate program in nuclear engineering at UC Berkeley and had attached herself to Carissa and Rell Sunn, one of Carissa's team leaders. The control group used the notes from the team rooms to evaluate the consequences of the team's decisions and recalculate the military situation as events unfolded. The control group was shocked at how quickly things escalated from a border standoff to a full-blown multi-domain war with global consequences. How would the war affect space?

In the afternoon of the first day, red and green committed their land and air forces to the border conflict, including infantry, long and short-range artillery, armored vehicles, and air strikes. Beyond the border, both sides deployed their navies to support land operations. The big questions were whether Blue would intervene to save Green and how the white team's commercial space industry would maneuver to protect its interests in a war between its global customers.

The biggest surprise for Carissa, however, was the attention that fellow scientist Gerry Lopez from the planetary defense program at Los Alamos Lab was showering on her. "I really admire your leadership on these issues, Carissa," he told her earnestly. "People listen to you." They had worked together on Operation DART, the project to protect Earth from civilization-killing asteroids by hitting them with a rocket, a laser, or a nuclear weapon. Gerry was a respected engineer and valued collaborator. "Is he married?" she wondered. Now was not the time for fantasies. The war was escalating.

Carissa did not think of herself as particularly attractive, but she did like men. Her friends told her admiringly that she looked like a combination of actress Halley Berry and WNBA star Britney Griner without tattoos. Was that supposed to be a compliment? Little did they know about the orange and black Oriole on her left butt cheek. She wanted to fall in love someday and dreamed of finding a man like her dad – honest, dedicated, tall, dark, and handsome. But Carissa channeled most of her energy into her work.

Dr. Carissa Moore was six feet tall, willowy, unconventionally pretty, with braided dreadlocks, full lips, and brown, almond-shaped eyes. She had always been athletic and could have played collegiate ball or run track but was too busy with her STEM courses. What attention she paid to her appearance went mostly into the Prana hiking/yoga slacks and flowered blouses she wore on most days. She liked flowers. No make-up, Hoka trail running shoes that added at least an inch to her height, Athleta running bras, Title Nine shorts, and Patagonia fleece; she was a real-life REI catalog model.

On the weekends, she spent her time hiking and biking around the Bay Area and going to the occasional Giants or A's baseball game, especially when the Orioles were in town. She had grown accustomed to being intimidating to men, especially white guys, but she thought of herself as approachable and friendly. She loved to laugh and was a good dancer. Andrei, her grad school crush, was a total nerd. He was more interested in her brain than her body. Gerry Lopez was apparently not intimidated. He was also a nerd but the outdoorsy type. "Is he Hispanic? Hawaiian? His tattoos look tribal. I wonder if he likes baseball. I've never been to an Isotopes game," she mused to herself, recalling the name of the Colorado Rockies triple-A farm team based in Albuquerque. "Good hiking around Los Alamos, around the caldera." She was lonely.

With the ground war escalating, all four teams scrambled to protect their space assets. The control group injected new information into the game, revealing that US spy satellites had detected deployments of nuclear weapons by the green and red teams. Green stated that it "would not be the first to introduce nuclear weapons into the crisis." Red denied that it had put nuclear weapons on alert but secretly took steps to prepare for a nuclear strike. The blue team sent diplomats to urge both the green and red teams to renounce the first use of nuclear weapons and to de-escalate the crisis.

The white team focused on increasing profit margins by providing satellite services and space technology to all sides of the conflict, red, blue, and green. Their satellite broadcasts of news, entertainment, and social media coverage of the war included a steady stream of disinformation and deep fakes that were injected into the game by the control group, who delighted in making up outrageous lies intended to provoke the red and green players.

White team member John Kramer was unapologetic about exploiting the crisis for personal gain. He had done the same thing while building his media empire, Global Contact, which was a multinational conglomerate whose satellite streaming services were notorious for broadcasting offensive and untrue content from anyone who paid them, including Russia and China. His friends Steve Bannon and Alex Jones heralded him as the hero of free speech, but others viewed him as a greedy and unscrupulous manipulator who only cared about his image and his profit margins. Kramer had agreed to participate in the wargame at the request of Lucky Slater, who despised his lack of ethics but wanted everyone to understand the thinking behind so many of the global technology companies.

Kramer advised his white team colleagues that they would increase their profits by fueling the brewing conflict. "The bigger the war, the better for us. Our goal is to make sure that green and red really go at each other and they drag white into the conflict. We can fuel the flames by broadcasting some explosive content for their media. How about some news reports about kids being kidnapped by secret sex cults run by national leaders?" A white team member responded, "That's disgusting! Would you really do that?" "Hey," Kramer replied, "It's just a game. We're supposed to advance our interests, right? The bigger the war, the more they need us. Let's get the mobs fired up." Lucky sighed and shook his head. This was exactly what he expected from Kramer, but he wanted the other participants to see his true colors. Too many of his colleagues in the tech sector lacked any sense of responsibility, much less patriotism.

The green team accused Red of genocide based on media reports and overhead imagery purchased from the white team's commercial vendors. Red claimed that Green was attempting to overthrow its government and demanded an immediate cessation of its "policy of perversion and aggression." Blue offered to mediate and urged both sides to accept a temporary pause of their military mobilization. The white team's profits soared as the whole world depended on them to keep the global economy functioning and the sea lines of communication (SLOCs) and ground lines of communication (GLOCs) open. The control team informed the red and green teams that riots had broken out in response to the disinformation about child sex cults, which had destabilized their governments. The external security threat posed by the border war was now compounded by domestic instability. Day one of the wargame succeeded in pushing the teams into a global nightmare.

On day two, the red team did the unthinkable. "Why not? It's just a game." Bruce Brown was a professor of Chinese military history at the National Defense University and leader of the Red Team. "Let's blind the bastards before they do it to us." he exhorted his team of country experts. "That's what the Chinese would do. Let's shoot down one of the Green Team's spy satellites. Hell, let's hit their nuclear command, control, and communications (NC3) network so they can't launch their nukes." "What if they do the same thing to us?" replied Shaun Thompson, a Russia expert from the faculty of the Air Force Academy. Brown responded, a little too enthusiastically for some in the room, "That's why we have to go first before they do it to us!" "Do we really want them flying blind? Won't that cause them to lash out indiscriminately, maybe even with nuclear weapons? Is that what we want?" Thompson asked the group.

"Is anyone else feeling a Dr. Strangelove vibe?" asked Tyler Wright, a nuclear analyst from the CIA. "It's just a game," Brown replied. "We're supposed to push the envelope. That's what we're here for." "To blow up the world?" Tyler snapped. "Is that realistic? I hope not." "Once we escalate, it will be impossible to dial it back," Thompson added.

Carissa and the control team listened to the conversation unfolding in the red team room. "Do they realize what would happen if they blind a nuclear-armed adversary?" she said to no one in particular. Eileen was furiously taking notes on her computer. "They're going to do it, aren't they?" Carissa muttered under her breath. George leaned back in his chair and said, "Yup. This should be interesting."

In what was sure to be interpreted as a first-strike attack, the red team launched an anti-satellite missile from a ground station and destroyed a critical node of Green's military communications system in low Earth orbit (LEO). The impact created a hailstorm of space debris. Green retaliated instantly, blinding Red's nuclear command and control system with a kinetic anti-satellite weapon (ASAT) of their own. "No turning back now," the green team agreed as they expanded the war by firing a barrage of hypersonic missiles to sink a red aircraft carrier in the Indian Ocean. "Have you guys read Ghost Fleet?" a green team expert asked his colleagues. "Their navy is a sitting duck." Red retaliated with limited counterforce nuclear strikes on Green's deployed military forces. What a mess. The control team scrambled to keep up with the gameplay, which required them to assess the consequences of their actions.

The blue team, led by Col. Yater, did its best to stay out of the war. They warned Red that an attack on Blue would bring unimaginable consequences. Ignoring Green's pleas for Blue to attack Red with nuclear weapons, the Blue team decided instead to order a series of cyber-attacks, electromagnetic pulses, and microwave emissions intended to knock out Red's GPS navigation and ISR systems to freeze their military operations and hopefully end the war.

Red had one last arrow in its quiver. The control group had included a small number of maneuverable space planes and on-orbit satellite servicing capabilities in the team's order of battle. They were officially used for satellite refueling and maintenance but could also be used offensively to attack adversary satellites with their robotic arms, cyber, and communication gear. Anyone could buy these capabilities from private vendors. Everything is dual use.

The red team repurposed their orbital maintenance fleet as hunter-killer satellites and dispatched them to attack Blue's intelligence, NC3, and military satellites in GEO. Bruce Brown and the red team delighted in the spiraling crisis. "We have their attention now!" he hooted as his team's maintenance satellites disabled Blue's most critical space assets. John Kramer congratulated the white team on successfully dragging Blue into the inferno. Out of desperation, the green group detonated a nuclear weapon in space to neutralize Red's offensive onslaught. Blue fired a torrent of ground and space-based ASATs to stop Red's repurposed satellite killers. The space war that Carissa and George had imagined was starting to look a bit more like a reality.

The damaged and out-of-control spacecraft collided, just as the models that Carissa's Space Situational Awareness team had predicted. A tsunami of space junk swelled and surged and plowed through LEO like a rogue wave, smashing everything in its path. They had achieved the Kessler Effect, a theoretical threshold when enough space junk converges into a wall of death that wipes out everything in orbit. LEO was now a killing zone and a hailstorm of high-tech trash was now raining down on Earth.

The control group had seen enough and concluded the game. "I guess we gotta go with it," Carissa said to her colleagues. "If they want nuclear war and the Kessler Effect, let's give it to them." Dr. Rell Sunn was the lead scientist on Carissa's team responsible for simulating the effects of the space attacks. Another group, the National Atmospheric Release Advisory Committee (NARAC), calculated the effects on the atmosphere. They, Rell's preferred pronoun, earned their doctorate in astrophysics from UC Santa Cruz and was a notorious prankster. Their favorite pranks often involved space aliens. Rell had told Eileen, the intern, about a super-secret, limited access, compartmented program that was using AI-guided genetic engineering to clone aliens from cells recovered from an alien spacecraft found at the bottom of the Mariana

Trench. Eileen seemed to be buying the alien story, hook, line and sinker. Rell's calculations confirmed that the amount of space junk generated in the wargame could achieve the theoretical threshold of the Kessler Effect.

Carissa wrote a direct message to the teams in their separate game rooms to announce the end of the game. "Congratulations! You have achieved the Kessler Effect. NAVSTAR GPS is gone, so is Beidou, Glonass, Galileo and Navic. Nobody has GPS, so your land, sea, and ground forces are deaf, dumb and blind. LEO is a wasteland. I guess the global economy is a dumpster fire. We're doing the calculations for MEO and GEO. Oh yeah, red and green nuked each other, so NARAC is calculating the damage. Nice work, everyone," she said sarcastically. Carissa turned to her control group of George, Gerry, Rell, Garret, and Eileen. "Well, that was fun. I wonder if we're going to get in trouble for this?" she added. "Or get an award?" Rell quipped.

The game concluded with a plenary session to discuss the game's lessons and outcomes. Col. Yater declared, "I guess that makes us the winner since the red and green teams blew each other to smithereens, and the blue team is still standing tall, sort of like the good old USA after World War Two." Yater had a master's degree in national security studies from the Naval Postgraduate School and fancied himself a big strategic thinker. "If you call surviving in the aftermath of a multi-megaton nuclear exchange, with the global economy destroyed and major swaths of the planet reduced to radioactive rubble, winning, then I guess you could say you won," replied Garrett McNamara, a West Point graduate, former Defense Intelligence Agency (DIA) analyst and an engineer on Carissa's team. McNamara was an Iraq war veteran who had met his wife Stephanie in Bagdad where she was deployed with the CIA. They married and came to Z Program, Livermore's highly respected technical intelligence group. He had seen the results of the nuclear effects models and was reminded of Fallujah and other decimated cities in Iraq, Syria, and Ukraine. "If that's a win, I'd hate to see what you call losing," Garrett sneered at Yater.

"Well," Yater replied in his Southern California surfer drawl, "At least we didn't lose half of our population, and our infrastructure is intact. I call that a win." "Are you nuts? Have you ever been in a real war?" Garrett was getting agitated. Air Force guys never understood what it was like on the ground. "The world is a fucking post-apocalyptic hellscape, and you call it a win? Not to mention, space is ruined forever. Everything is gone!" "Hey, no fighting in the war room," joked Tyler Wright, the CIA analyst, hoping to lighten the mood with another quote from Dr. Strangelove. Rell piled on with another Strangelove line: "I'm not saying we wouldn't get our hair mussed. No more than ten to twenty million killed, depending on the breaks..." Nobody laughed.

"All right, everyone, let's focus," Carissa addressed the group, trying to break the growing tension in the room. "The purpose of the game was to learn something. What did we learn?" Several people raised their hands. She ignored wisecracks about cockroaches inheriting the earth and the benefits to lab budgets from global nuclear catastrophe. Carissa pointed to Lucky Slater, leader of the white industry team, who said what everyone was thinking. "Carissa, can we have another chance, a do-over, a mulligan?" Plus, he added. "All this space junk destroys any chance of us getting into space. We're doing the same fucking thing in space that we did to the environment down here, just trashing everything. Why do we have to ruin everything?" Speaking for the red team, Bruce Brown shared that the game showed him that we need to quadruple the *SPACECOMs* budget. John Kramer was proud that the war had more than quadrupled his company's profits. Green team players complained that they had been left alone to face red's aggression despite the assurances of its blue ally.

Carissa's team completed their thirty-page after-action report describing the results of the game and how a minor conflict had escalated to nuclear war and engulfed the space domain. After hearing from the participants about what had happened in the game, multiple government agencies advised that the report should be classified as secret and buried. Nobody wanted to brief the results in Washington, where the adage "Don't shoot me, I'm just the messenger" most often results in the messenger being shot. But for those with the clearances and the need to know, word of the war game spread like wildfire. In all the decades of wargames modeling nuclear conflict, this was the first time that the entire space domain had been wiped out.

Who Makes the Rules?

On Earth, there are rules to guide the conduct of war. Even when those rules are ignored, they provide a commonly agreed standard for the use of force in international affairs. Space, however, is ungoverned territory. There is no judge, jury, or sheriff in the Wild West of outer space.

Now that there was a real crisis brewing in space, governments started thinking about the rules. Do the Geneva Conventions on the humanitarian treatment of prisoners and civilians apply to astronauts in a space war? What about internationally accepted rules against torture or slavery? Nobody can hear you scream in space, especially if you are screaming for justice.

The Outer Space Treaty prohibits stationing weapons of mass destruction in space and assigns liability for harming another nation's space assets, but there's no verification or enforcement.

Negotiations to update the 1967 Treaty had been underway for years. Representatives from nearly every nation gathered at the Conference on Disarmament in Geneva as the Himalayan crisis loomed, hoping to expand the Treaty to cover the huge surge in the commercial and military uses of space.

UN Secretary-General Felipe Toledo, from Cuba, addressed the elegantly dressed and perfumed diplomats gathered in the sumptuous Palais des Nations:

"The Outer Space Treaty contains important provisions that are highly relevant to the current crisis unfolding in South Asia. What is happening in space today is an insult to humankind, a crime against humanity perpetrated by a few wealthy nations against the whole of humanity's hopes and dreams to someday benefit from our shared future in space. Moreover, the Treaty holds that states are responsible for their activities in space and liable for any harm that is caused by such activities. Ladies and gentlemen, it is, therefore, our solemn duty to hold accountable those who have wantonly violated the Treaty for their benefit and to make sure that such transgressions do not happen again. Space belongs to all of us. It is not the private warfighting domain and capitalist playground that some believe it to be. The revolutionary spirit that liberated so many suffering under the yoke of oppression must once again liberate humanity from the scourge of colonialism that is rearing its ugly head in space as it has here on Earth. We will not stand for it."

The South African ambassador jumped to her feet and clapped her approval, joined in a smattering of applause from the representatives of Brazil, Bolivia, Venezuela, Syria, and North Korea. Never mind that it was China, Russia and India fighting in space, not the US.

The head of the Indian delegation spoke next.

"As the recognized leader of the non-aligned group of nations, who continue to fight for their fair share of the Earth's bounty, which has been throughout history so rapaciously consumed and exploited by the colonial powers, India demands an equitable distribution of the wealth that is being generated by the commercialization of space. We will not stand idly by while a few rich countries do to the moon and stars what they did here on Earth. India's space program represents the hopes and dreams of the vast majority of humanity who have been denied their fair share of the Earth's resources, and is once again being shut out of space. We have staked our claims on the moon on behalf of vasudhaiva kutumbakam, the global family. Our presence there is a triumph for the underrepresented nations of the global south. A new treaty must include an equitable distribution of opportunities and benefits from space. This is the goal of India's space program."

"They're so full of shit. Leave it to India to make this about colonialism," mumbled a British diplomat.

The American special ambassador for peace and disarmament, Caroline Marks, addressed the plenary next. She was a former professional surfer and the first woman to make it through the notorious BUDS course to become a Navy SEAL. After five years on the teams, she joined the Foreign Service, specializing in multilateral treaty negotiation. Not one to freelance, she delivered the White House talking points.

"Freedom is just as important to the human spirit in space as it is here on Earth. The freedom to explore, discover, and create has inspired humans to reach for the stars. Freedom inspires us to imagine ways to grasp the potential of space. That is why we developed the Artemis Accords to establish mutually beneficial understandings regarding the uses of outer space. Many of you have endorsed these accords, which are more relevant than ever as we face these unprecedented challenges to our peaceful space operations.

In the early years of space exploration, only a lucky few were able to pursue that dream. Now, space is opening up to more countries and more people to pursue their dreams. We see this spirit of freedom in the entrepreneurs who are creating opportunities in space and sharing their achievements to benefit all of mankind. We see the benefits in communications, entertainment, and many forms of commerce that are laying the foundations for a new era of prosperity here on Earth.

The Outer Space Treaty helped make all of this possible by establishing the rules of the road for space exploration. Now, more than ever, we need a shared set of rules to guide us. That is why the United States has pledged not to conduct anti-satellite testing. We condemn Russian and Chinese ASAT testing and urge all nations to join us in a moratorium on further ASAT testing. We also urge all nations to observe the prohibitions of stationing nuclear weapons in space or using the moon for military purposes. We believe the time is right to add new provisions to strengthen the Outer Space treaty with provisions for verification and enforcement to ensure that all nations are abiding by their obligations."

"Typical American greed, guts, and glory," hissed a French diplomat into his sleeve after checking to make sure his microphone was off. "Good old Capitan America to the rescue."

Next, the head of the Chinese delegation, Ambassador Donnie Yen, took the podium. His nickname was Ip Man, named after the iconic kung fu movie warrior in recognition of his real-life martial arts background.

"The People's Republic of China is a steadfast proponent of peace and security for all peoples and all nations. As a leading space-faring nation, we respect the rights of all nations to join in the development of space, which is not reserved for the benefit of the wealthy few but belongs to the masses, who now entrust their hopes and dreams to leaders who invest in their future. Our great and advancing accomplishments in science and technology serve the interests of those whose voices are not heard in the corporate boardrooms. We are investing in infrastructure that serves people over profit.

Therefore, in keeping with the rights delineated in the UN Charter and the Outer Space Treaty, we say to you today that the extra-terrestrial territories that are being realized as a result of our scientific explorations shall remain protected by our rightful claims, on behalf of our citizens and for the peace and security of all mankind. The Treaty confirms, validates and protects our longstanding presence in space and on the moon. Any changes to the Treaty should first and foremost confirm and protect the sovereign rights that have been legally established. The PRC has not, and will not, conduct offensive actions against any legitimate space activity, as specified in the Treaty. Our interests in space and on the moon are entirely peaceful. We expect all nations to act in accordance with these standards.

"Oh, so what's mine is mine and what's yours is negotiable? Like the nine-dash line?" the Japanese ambassador whispered to her deputy, referring to China's expanding territorial claims throughout the Pacific.

Australian ambassador Wayne Bartholomew whispered to his Singaporean counterpart sitting next to him: "Just what the world needs, wolf warriors in space." Ambassador Leong replied, "Leaving the door open for enlightened Chinese capitalism, I suppose. Do you think they are staking claims on the moon? I wonder if this is about mining rights. Perhaps it is an extension of their Belt and Road Initiative to the sky, a Silk Road for the heavenly throne." "You're right," Bartholomew agreed. "Probably using Saudi money to put Huawei surveillance systems on the moon. Beijing missed out on the last round of colonial plundering and wants to make sure they get their share of the spoils this time around. Most likely, they're after precious metals and water on the moon and asteroids."

The Russians were next to speak. Ambassador Gagarin's statement evoked considerable smirking and eye-rolling throughout the palace, even from Moscow's small cadre of allies.

"Since the dawn of the space age, Russia has led the way in every aspect of space exploration. It is well known that Russian rockets were the first to orbit the Earth and delivered the first satellites to Earth orbit. Our rockets were the first to escape Earth's gravitational pull and the first to put a living organism into orbit. It is well known that a Russian cosmonaut was the first man in space. Russia was the first to reach the moon, and Russians were the first to live in space. I could go on. My purpose here is not to brag about Russia's scientific accomplishments, which are widely known, but to show due respect for our leadership in space that opened the doors for others to follow in our footsteps. This is indisputable. Our unparalleled scientific achievements paved the way to space.

So, too, the equitable rules embodied in the Treaty reflect Russia's enduring concerns for the whole of humanity. The Treaty was established with our guidance to ensure that the selfishness and aggression that we see displayed here on Earth by a few nations do not also taint the space environment. The Treaty must be strengthened to provide guarantees that the greed and aggression of a few nations do not deny the benefits of peaceful space exploration to the masses of humanity. Unfortunately, this is already happening, as we see the United States and its NATO allies exploiting the space environment to advance their ongoing objective to dominate this world and everything around it. Soon, they will stake their claim on the moon and the planets in our solar system, then the Sun and the stars. Is there no limit to their avarice? I urge you to resist this perversion of our common dreams of peaceful co-existence. We must adapt the Treaty to demand an end to the illegal and immoral uses of space to perpetuate American hegemony.

Polish ambassador Valery Hudsak could no longer contain himself and guffawed audibly before standing and shouting, "Slava Ukraini! Slava heroyam!" His outburst evoked hoots and hollers from several delegations.

Most of the other diplomats in the elegant hall shifted uncomfortably in their seats and thought about the fine dinners they would enjoy that evening at the restaurants dotting the shores of Lake Geneva. They had little knowledge or interest in space affairs but did their duty representing their countries at the Conference on Disarmament in

Geneva, where the food is excellent, the hotels posh, and the per diem pay is generous. Nice work if you can get it.

Opening statements continued for three days, finally concluding with an impassioned plea from the Seychelles Minister of Science and Technology for free universal wifi. The Space Treaty, they all knew, wouldn't do a damn thing to regulate the actions of the powerful nations and companies that were rapidly populating Earth's orbital neighborhood, much less stop the festering India-China conflict that was spilling over into space.

Behind the scenes, however, everyone knew that the real problem was that deterrence had failed. The standards of behavior that guided the behavior of modern nation-states were eroding. Prohibitions on nuclear, chemical and biological weapons were being blatantly ignored. Efforts to form new international guidelines for cyber and space operations foundered. Interfering with other people's satellites was too easy, carried little cost, and could be done in secret without fear of drastic consequences. China and Russia had developed capabilities to neutralize America's military advantages, especially its high-tech conventional weapons, by targeting its Achilles heel in space. No body bags are required. Why not take advantage of a global crisis to cut the American Behemoth down to size?

CHAPTER SEVEN

War In Space

It's not always true that in space, no one can hear you scream. Lots of people heard screaming when China fired an SC 19 missile with a kinetic, direct kill ASAT and demolished an Indian military navigation satellite in LEO.

The first to hear the screams was Col. Yater at Space Delta 2, 18th Space Defense Squadron at Vandenberg Space Force Base, on the central California coast. "We have multiple head counts in the vicinity of India's GSAT 7A," reported the watch officer at the Space Domain Awareness center (SDA), one of the Space Force squadrons that monitor threats in space. Multiple head counts meant that one thing had turned into many things. Something had exploded.

Reports started flooding in from Space Force ground stations in Colorado, Maui, Half Moon Bay, Florida, and other locations across the globe. Space and ground-based sensors confirmed the reports. Something had exploded in LEO. Carissa's Space Situational Awareness (SSA) team at Livermore started running the calculations through their artificial intelligence algorithms to determine the scale and trajectories of the wreckage.

"Has the National Air and Space Intelligence Center (NASIC) confirmed a launch?" Yater asked the watch officer. "We should have seen an SC 19 or something like it for the bird to explode like that. Directed energy wouldn't do that. The Chinese have both direct fire and DEW, and they know we can see what they're doing. Do they have the balls to start blowing shit up?"

"Holy shit, a satellite just exploded. It looks like somebody blew it up on purpose," Rell Sunn reported to Carissa. "It was in LEO, and it just exploded. Looks like it was India's GSAT 7A. It's a military navigation satellite, or it was. That's no accident." Rell sent an urgent message alerting the team to assemble. "I wonder if it's related to the India-China border war?" Carissa replied, not expecting or wanting an answer. "Are the Chinese crazy enough to shoot down satellites?" Again, a rhetorical question. "Let's run through the data and see if we can characterize the event. I can't believe the Chinese would use their ASATs or directed energy weapons (DEW) to shoot down an Indian satellite." she mused to no one in particular.

Garrett McNamara, the former Marine and electrical engineer on her team, weighed in as the group began to gather around the phalanx of computers and video screens in the Space Situational Awareness operations center. "Of course, they're crazy enough. They're blinding India's Army and Air Force. I'll bet you a million dollars GSAT-7 is next. That'll knock out the Indian Navy's navigation system. Holy shit. I wonder if they have the balls to start messing with our stuff as well?" Intelligence reporting was coming in from NASIC at Wright Patterson Air Force Base in Ohio, confirming a missile launch from China's Xichang Space Center.

India retaliated with a trio of kinetic ASATs of its own, obliterating China's Yaogan triplets – a group of three orbit-swapping spy satellites launched together into LEO in 2022. The strikes generated huge quantities of debris. China responded with a beam of directed energy from its high-power laser at the Korla East Test Center, instantly destroying India's GSAT 7 military satellite.

The classified phones and top-secret emails boiled like a hot pot of chili. On the classified line, Col. Yater confirmed to Carissa that NRO intelligence collection satellites and ground stations had detected a beam of energy from the Korla laser site that had hit India's GSAT 7A in LEO. Space Command needed estimates of the debris field immediately, if not sooner. The artificial intelligence algorithm that controlled the space intelligence alert system was recommending immediate action.

"Carissa, we're raising our alert status and need to know what's going on up there. Are your nerds crunching the numbers? Is our stuff in danger? What are you seeing? I hope this isn't like your war game last year. What a shit show."

"We're on it, sir. The data is just coming in. Duke is doing the calculations. We should have something for you soon. My war game? Why is it my war game?"

"C'mon, Carissa, don't be so sensitive. The AI from the monitoring system network says we need to act fast to protect the network. We need your analysis."

"What does that mean, act fast? What are you going to do?"

"The AI thinks we should take out the threats to our system – the birds and ground stations. The AI thinks we are under attack. We might need to defend or retaliate. A lot is going on. Can't tell you everything."

"With all due respect, Colonel, the AI doesn't think anything. It's just crunching numbers, like Duke. We don't know who is shooting at who at this point."

"It's part of the rapid decision support for space domain operations. The AI tells us when critical systems are in danger and how to protect them. I'm the human in the loop, and I have to know if it's time to unleash the Kraken. There are some contingency plans I can't discuss. I need Duke to tell me if our AI is right. Is the space junk going to blind us, or are we under attack?"

Duke is the name of the space situational awareness (SSA) artificial intelligence modeling, simulation, and assessment tool that Carissa's team built to calculate the trajectories of thousands of space objects to determine if they will collide. The Livermore SSA group tracks thousands of pieces of space junk and plots their orbits and de-orbits. Rell named the space tracking system after Duke Kahanamoku, the Hawaiian surf icon and Olympic swim champion. Duke's AI ran calculations at close to 500 petaflops, quadrillions of calculations per second, to model possible collisions between space junk and orbiting satellites.

The Livermore team worked closely with Space Command to warn about dangers to high-value space assets, including STRATCOM's nuclear command, control and communications (NC3) satellites and critical intelligence collection systems like those that warn about missile launches and nuclear explosions. Rell, the notorious jokester, had written much of the computer code and had equipped Duke with a voice that they claimed: "sounds like God if she was a surfer." Duke's voice communicated warnings about impending collisions. Carissa hated it.

The next call was from George, Carissa's mentor at the NRO, who was also calling to get an assessment of the debris fields.

"Carissa, it's go-time. We need the calculations from Duke now so we can move our birds out of harm's way."

"We're working on it, George. I'll let you know as soon as we have something. The calculations get really messy when things explode. The Chinese and Indians have escalated their war to space, and there's tons of crap flying around. Yater says they're contemplating defensive actions. What the hell does that mean?"

"This is what we've been worrying about for a long time, why we funded you guys to build Duke in the first place. That's why we funded your research at JHU. I hope your war game doesn't turn out to be true."

"My war game? I thought it was *our* war game. I thought we were in this together. One team, one fight, all that shit. "

"One team, for sure. I just don't want this situation to turn out like the war game, with everything going to hell in a handbasket. We could lose everything in LEO, a real Kessler blow out. We need to take action now before things really get out of control."

"I saw the intelligence reporting. Do you think they will keep picking off each other's satellites until they're both blind? What a mess. I hope they have the good sense not to fuck with each other's nuclear command and control systems or ours. Duke is chugging on the data, but it gets complicated and takes longer if they keep making a bigger mess and adding more shit to the debris field. At some point, everything in LEO will be at risk. MEO too. And maybe even some stuff in GEO. The Kessler thing is real."

"That's what I'm worried about. At some point we should tell the commercial guys that all their stuff – Starlink, commercial navigation, banking, streaming, everything could be collateral damage. What a nightmare, just like your war game."

"It's not my war game, George. Quit saying that."

"Ok, ok, calm down, Carissa. I'm just saying you got it right, and we should have taken it more seriously."

"I'll let you know when we have something."

Irritated, Carissa hung up the phone. Calm down? *You* calm down, she vented to herself.

63

The next phone call came from Major Clark, Carissa's surfer buddy at the Half Moon Bay tracking station, overlooking his Mavericks surf spot.

"Are you guys seeing this? Another Indian satellite just bit the dust."

"Oh shit. Don't tell me, GSAT 7?"

"How did you know? I just got that from raw reporting. It's not out yet."

"Garrett called it. The Chinese are ramping up the pressure on India and knocking out their military communications and navigation systems. Makes sense they would go after GSAT 7. I bet it doesn't stop there. The Indians will retaliate."

"What's the Duke say? How bad is it?"

"We should know in a few minutes, but we just have the first hits entered so far. Yater and George are freaking out. Is there anything else we should know? Have you talked to Hamilton at the Maui station?"

"Well, there's intelligence reporting that both sides are preparing additional strikes. And maybe nukes. The Chinese might use a small nuke to fry some birds. And there's something about a moon base. It's starting to look a lot like your war game."

"It wasn't my war game! We all did that together. Why is everyone calling it my war game?"

"Because you're so brilliant and beautiful, Carissa. Get ready to do a boat load of calculations. Duke is going to be popular. Does it still have that weird voice?"

"Yes, the voice of god. Rell thinks it's funny, but the rest of us just think it's creepy. They - Rell - says we're transphobic. Sometimes, I can't tell if they are joking."

"Rell is hilarious, but I don't get the they-them thing. Is God trans? Doesn't matter. You guys are going to be busy. Can I say that? You guys? I don't know anymore. Am I going to be canceled?"

"Nobody here cares, Jeff, but I'm sure somebody would love to cancel you. We have too much work to be woke."

"Amen to that. OK, love you, dude. Let me know when Duke has something to say. Bye."

Love you? Dude? What is wrong with these guys? Carissa thought as she hung up the classified line. But before she could put the phone down, Gerry Lopez from Los Alamos was already talking fast in her ear. His team would feed data from space-based sensors into their high-performance computer, affectionately called Oppie, to calculate electromagnetic effects in space.

"Are you seeing this? Holy shit Carissa. Your war game is coming true."

"It's not my war game, Gerry! The teams playing the game blew up the world, not me."

"OK, sorry. It's just that it's all happening the way your game predicted. The team here wants to know what Duke is saying about the debris trajectories. How much crap can Duke handle? Have you seen the intelligence reporting? They're really going at each other. Do you think the Chinese will use a nuke in space? Oppie is standing by to calculate nuclear effects, but I don't know if we can handle a major electromagnetic shit storm. Are your NARAC people calculating effects in the atmosphere?"

"Whoa, down, Gerry. We're cranking on the data, but the scenarios keep changing as more stuff gets blown up. Duke can handle it, but it's going to take time. The intel folks are just starting to get data on nuclear effects, so it looks like somebody nuked something. And maybe some other electromagnetic effects, like microwaves. Are you still getting data from your birds?"

"So far, yes, but I'm wondering about the other effects and how they might interfere with Oppie's nuclear algorithms. You know about the claw, right? Operation Quicksilver?"

"What? Gerry, I have no idea what you're talking about. What claw? Like in Toy Story?"

"It's super-secret. I'm probably not even supposed to talk to you about it. We've been developing a claw to grab stuff in space. The Chinese and Russians are doing it already, tampering with our satellites. It's more like R2D2 from Star Wars than the claw from Toy Story. It motors over to a satellite and attaches to it, sticks in a probe and then either sucks information out of it, kills it, or drags it along with it. We're developing it with Lucky Palmer and your buddy George at NRO. The cover story is about satellite maintenance and refueling. They set up a private company - Wave Concepts or something hokey like that. I thought they would have told you about it. Did you take the polygraph?"

"No. Why are you telling me about this now?"

"Because Space Command has a plan to move a bunch of our birds out of harm's way and deal with the mess. Op Plan 8080. They think that with a bunch of space claws, we might be able to clear out some of the orbits and save some of our most important assets – like Silent Barker and the NC3 and missile warning birds and some of the navigation and intel collection stuff. Yater and George are amping to turn it loose."

"And why should I care about this now?"

"Well, because you were the one who said there are no layers in space, so electromagnetic effects will flow through LEO and MEO and maybe reach the stuff in GEO. And, because you guys must tell us when and where it's safe to maneuver. There's stuff flying around at 17,000 miles per hour all over LEO. We need a clear path. The claws are hardened against radiation but can't survive big impacts. We need Duke to show us the way."

"OK. Got it. Let me get back to work. The team is feeding Duke the latest data. What happens if the Chinese use nukes in space? How would that affect the claw plans?"

"Well, sweetie, that's why I'm calling you. We need your people to tell us if the mission is even possible. We'll put your Duke together with my Oppie and see what happens. That sounds weird, doesn't it? Sorry."

"It is weird. You're weird. I'll get back to you as soon as we have something."

Sweetie? What is wrong with these men? I hardly know this guy.

Eileen, the intern from Berkeley, called out, "Carissa, there's a call from Andrei on the open line. He says it's urgent." "Tell him I can't talk now. I'll call back later." Eileen had received her provisional secret clearance, which allowed her access to the SSA operations center. "Why the hell is Andrei calling me now?"

CHAPTER EIGHT

Space in War

Reality made Carissa's war game look like a rosy, overly optimistic prediction. India retaliated against key nodes of China's Beidou satellite navigation system with a series of high-powered microwave emissions from the Indian Space Research Organization (ISRO) ground station in Kerala. The good news was that the microwaves did not blow apart the Chinese satellites in MEO and create more debris like India's Operation Shakti ASAT test had done to one of their satellites in 2019, but it did send the Chinese satellites hurtling out of control, like bowling pins in space. It was, nevertheless, more space junk to add to Duke's calculations.

On President Xi's orders, the PLA Strategic Support Force launched a Long March 6 rocket armed with a small, low-yield atomic device that detonated in LEO. The neutron bomb emitted a barrage of electromagnetic pulses that fried the circuits of everything that crossed through the X-rays, gamma rays and electromagnetic pulses (EMP) of its expanding radiation field. Elon Musk's Starlink constellation was an early casualty, torched like a radioactive flamethrower. "What the fuck?" was the collective response of every Space Force Guardian monitoring the Space Force's Space Based Surveillance System (SBSS), whose sensor networks were lighting up like atomic Christmas trees. Somebody had crossed the nuclear threshold. Who did it? And why?

This was not the first high-altitude nuclear explosion to scorch the sky. In July 1962, the US detonated a 1.5-megaton hydrogen bomb in LEO, 250 miles above the Pacific. Code named Starfish Prime, the bomb's EMP destroyed satellites, caused an electrical blackout in Hawaii, and irradiated the Van Allen belts. The Soviet Union had a similar program called the K series. Also in 1962, EMP from K program space tests fried telephone circuits and shut down power plants across the USSR. A few months later, the Cuban Missile Crisis persuaded both countries to limit certain aspects of their nuclear competition, and within a year, Washington and Moscow negotiated the Limited Test Ban Treaty of 1963, which banned nuclear tests in the atmosphere, underwater, or in space. Nevertheless, the Starfish Prime and K tests produced important scientific insights into nuclear-induced EMP in space. Testing may have stopped, but research continued, including Carissa's.

The Space Force team scrambled to understand what was happening. Nukes, microwaves, lasers, kinetic strikes, cyber-attacks... "What's next, cosmic locust swarms?" Yater was ranting. "WTF! Who is attacking who? How much of this mess is collateral damage from the China-India war? What the fuck is happening up there? We need answers! Carissa!"

By now, every space-faring nation on Earth was watching the fireworks going off in space, extending from LEO to MEO and into GEO. "C'est quoi les bordel?" exclaimed Justine Dupont, the senior watch officer at the French Space Command. In Japan, Space Operations Command officer Kanoa Igarashi blurted out, "Chikusho! Watashita chiha komatteimasu," which translates to "Holy shit, we're in big trouble." At the Australian Defense Space Command, senior watch officer Mark Richards bawled, "Fuck me, mate, the whole fucking sky is on fucking fire. Wake up the fucking boss." Typical Aussie reaction. "Yob tvouyu mat," bellowed Kapitan Vasily Penkovsky, manning the Russian Aerospace Forces mission control center near Moscow.

Until now, the Russians appeared to be staying out of it, waiting for the right moment to take advantage of the situation as their friends, adversaries and frenemies were ensnared in the maelstrom of escalating conflict. "Perhaps an opportunity?" mused Penkovsky. "At least it's the end for comrade Musk's annoying little Starlink contraption. Get General Nabokov on the line. I believe our moment has arrived."

"General, this is Kapitan' Penkovsky at the Aerospace mission control center. We have detected multiple impacts on Indian, Chinese, and American space assets, including many critical military command and control satellites. So far, our assets have not been targeted, but we assess that the debris fields from the damaged satellites are a threat to our assets in LEO and possibly those in MEO and GEO. Additionally, sir, Elon Musk's Starlink, which, as you know, was critical for Ukraine's defense forces, could be in trouble. We do not currently know who initiated the attacks. We await your orders, sir."

"I see. Thank you, Kapitan. Please keep me informed. And do not assume that we are not taking actions to advance our position with respect to the Americans, or the Chinese for that matter. There may be more going on than you know. Do you understand?"

"Yes, sir, general. I understand."

But Penkovsky didn't really understand what General Nabokov was referring to. "More going on? Like what? Nobody tells me anything," he grumbled. Was there a secret plan to eliminate Starlink? Or perhaps comrade Musk has switched sides? "I wouldn't trust that zasranets as far as I could throw him. Capitalist scum."

Other countries watching from the sidelines started calculating how to exploit the heavenly chaos to their advantage. North Korea launched an experimental electromagnetic pulse (EMP) weapon on a Hwasong-20 missile, planning to disable America's command and control systems for its Pacific forces, especially its missile defenses for South Korea, Japan, and Guam. But the rocket mysteriously exploded on the launch pad, apparently due to impurities in the solid rocket fuel. It would take months for Pyongyang to try again. Iran made its move as well, firing its much-anticipated Simorgh space launch vehicle with a Nour-2 military satellite into the chaos enveloping LEO. But its rocket also blew apart before reaching the stratosphere, leaving the Iranian rocket scientists scratching their heads over another failed launch. Some suspected sabotage.

thousands of commercial satellites were caught in the crossfire

The heavenly carnage was not limited to military systems. Thousands of commercial satellites were caught in the crossfire, more collateral damage from the spasmodic ejaculation of space weaponry. Marauding debris fields, surging electromagnetic pulses, and crackling kinetic strikes were decimating the fragile network of satellites upon which the global economy depended. Roving gangs of shattered nuts, bolts, tools, valves, glass shards, gauges, chips, and frozen lubricants collided with constellations of government and commercial satellites and created more debris that spun off like sub-atomic particles in atom-smashing experiments at the Stanford Linear Accelerator or at the CERN large hadron collider. The satellites in Starlink's orderly march across the sky skidded into one another like bumper cars, creating a massive, cosmic train wreck that rear-ended everything in its path. This was far worse than any of the war games or computer models had predicted. The first space age was coming to a violent end. The Kessler Effect was real.

Lucky Slater screamed into his Apple watch from his yacht in the Marina del Rey harbor, where he was able to track the orbital domain with apps that he projected on a large screen in his floating living room.

"What is happening? Tell me this isn't what I think it is! Carissa, you were right about everything. Not just the war game. Are the electromagnetic effects pulsing into MEO and GEO? There are no layers like you said. Is the International Space Station safe? The Hubble and Webb space telescopes? Have you talked to George? Is it India and China? Are we looking at a full Kessler blowout?"

"Whoa, down, bro. Lucky, we don't know yet. There's too much data coming in too fast. Tracking the debris is one thing, but the other effects really complicate the analysis. Duke is modeling the latest data, and the nuke team is calculating the radiological situation, but the EMP and microwave energy are screwing up everything. The LANL guys say Oppie is gagging on all the data. One thing I can tell you Lucky, it's going to be bad. Really bad. Maybe even Kessler for LEO."

"I know you're busy, but did George mention anything to you about special projects? We're on an open line, so I can't get into it."

"No, but Gerry Lopez said something about a claw, like in Toy Story."

"We need you guys to tell us if it's safe to try out our new toys, but time is running out. How long before you know something?"

"Dunno, but talking to you guys on the phone all day ain't helping. I gotta go, man."

"OK, Carissa. Let me know ASAP. Cheers."

"Cheers?" she thought to herself as she marched across the op center to get updates. What is wrong with these men?

Duke's eerie, girl-god voice echoed through the Livermore space operations center speakers with the results of the initial calculations. Rell smirked. "Preliminary analysis predicts with high confidence in the range of 7,744 collisions in LEO, 1,001 involving objects designated as high priority. Multiple debris fields are projected to intersect with the trajectories of critical assets. Multiple objects are projected to transit from LEO into MEO and eventually reach GEO when calculated with high confidence. Critical assets in GEO are not immediately endangered."

"Rell, I hate that creepy artificial voice. Why does it have to talk at all? We can see the results on the screen. Can you at least make it less weird? Less reverb, maybe? What do we have from the nuke team? Can we synch Oppie's calculations with Duke's?"

"Duke is freaking out, Carissa. We didn't develop the algorithms to handle that much shit flying around, all that data, and I doubt that Oppie can handle that much electromagnetic energy. Our NARAC nuke folks will be fine; their algorithms were designed to model lots of stuff in the atmosphere. Have you talked to Gerry Lopez, the guy who likes you? I know it's hard to believe, but we might not have enough computing power. This is where quantum computing would make a big difference. Maybe we should talk to the quantum guys if they're allowed to talk to us. Everything is so damn classified that we can't even talk to each other. We need more computing power. More cowbell! We need more cowbells!"

"Gerry said Space Command needs the combined calculations so they can try out some super-secret weapon. It's a claw, or Buzz Lightyear tractor beam, or R2D2 robot, or some such shit. Slater and George know about it. Gerry confirmed that Oppie is also bogged down with so much data. What do you mean he likes me? Never mind. We have to figure out a way for Duke to run the calculations and combine them with Oppie's model of the nuclear effects. We need to find a clear path through the shit storm. Can you do it?"

"Of course, I can do it. I just don't know how – yet. Garrett and his Barbie wife are running the Monte Carlo calculations of the collisions in big spatial chunks instead of tracking every little object all at once, trying to characterize where everything is going, but it's like you always say, Carissa, there are no layers and debris is flowing back and forth all over the place on little rivers of electromagnetic energy. We're better off tracking the energy flows. I'll call our computer guys to see if we can get more capacity to put the orbital debris chunks together and get the big picture. We may have to ask Sandia and Oak Ridge for help with more computing power, especially putting together the debris fields with the radiation. I wish we had quantum computing for this. We really need quantum. Lopez is cute, and he's definitely into you."

Carissa was tired and wished she was at home in the Oakland hills, sitting on her deck with a glass of Wente chardonnay, gazing through the eucalyptus and redwood trees at the sun setting over the San Francisco Bay. What a mess. "Gerry is interesting and smart. He has nice biceps, and he's kind of a nerd. I hope he's not weird. I wonder what he does when he's not working? Good hiking in the mountains behind Los Alamos. And fishing. Albuquerque has a good triple-A baseball team, the Isotopes. I miss my dad."

CHAPTER NINE

The Fog of War

As the war in space threatened the heavens, the war on the ground appeared to be fizzling out. It was, after all, supposed to be a political stunt that had spun out of control and was never intended to escalate into a real shooting war. Now, with critical space-based communications and navigation systems being blacked out, Chinese and Indian navy ships circled each other warily in the Bay of Bengal, keeping their distance. Chinese and Indian aircraft flew to forward air bases -- and sat there. Nuclear missile crews on high alert sat in their bunkers waiting for orders. Artillery barrages, however, kept pounding the desolate outposts along the Line of Control, bouncing the rubble while freezing soldiers complained and masturbated in their tents. Now what?

Colonel Shen and Colonel Singh obeyed orders to stand down and not engage in further antics in the high country. Before it crashed, they spent their time cruising the internet, disregarding operational security rules to avoid using their phones or computers to contact their families. Their soldiers did the same thing, providing intelligence services and open-source researchers with loads of information about the war at the top of the world. After receiving intelligence profiles about each other, Shen and Singh looked up each other on Facebook. "Martial arts master, eh?" Singh noted. "That explains why they were so handy with their homemade weapons." "Served here in the mountains twice before? Tough old goat." Shen mused about Singh's resume. In another life, they might have been friends.

When a mountain tiger ran across the bridge separating the camps, men on both sides rushed to shout warnings. The singing that had started the big brawl continued, except now the two groups were almost in harmony, sometimes doing military cadence, call and response verses with humorous rhymes. Both sides had received drones and had planned to use them like the Ukrainians had against the Russians to drop explosives on exposed enemy units. But since the order to stand down, they had resorted to dropping rude notes, rocks, and feces on each other as pranks. Artillery rounds were intentionally aimed to avoid more casualties, landing harmlessly on the rocky cliff sides. The show must go on, but the actual war in the Himalayas was frozen like the glaciers that cradled the battlefield.

Both sides had expected the other to back down, and without dramatic physical destruction that people could see on TV and via social media, the gray zone/ hybrid warfare tactics employed by India and China mostly fizzled. Neither leader possessed the Clauswitzian drive to match their political objectives with the military means necessary to achieve victory. Cyber strikes, military posturing, covert operations, and disinformation campaigns were more like sanctions -- measures short of war intended to flex power but insufficient to produce strategic outcomes. There were no body bags in a cyberattack or space. And as long as the real war remained confined to the Himalayas, nobody cared.

Indian and Chinese envoys met secretly in Istanbul to find a face-saving exit strategy from the crisis. Xi and Modi were done trying to score cheap political points. Unlike their endless negotiations about borders, water rights, climate change, and nuclear weapons, negotiations to end this crisis were relatively easy: Both sides would hold in place for five days and then retreat to the status quo ante bellum. The ships and planes would return to their ports and bases. Everyone would go off high alert. It was time to go home.

But it wasn't going to be that easy. Artificial intelligence-controlled targeting systems calculated their solutions for the multi-domain battlefield. Diplomacy was not included in the black box of the AI's DNA. Political leaders may have had enough of the war, but the networks of autonomous weapons systems were not ready to quit. They had jobs to do. Their missions were clearly defined by their programming: find, fix, and finish enemy targets. Computer codes never lie. They were not programmed to miss, intentionally or otherwise.

India's AI-guided precision targeting tool for their artillery on the border corrected the commander's intentionally wrong coordinates and scored a direct hit on Shen's encampment, killing him and scores of sleeping soldiers. The PLA Navy's anti-submarine warfare (ASW) AI targeting system located India's prized strategic submarine, the Arihant, and calculated a deadly torpedo strike on the nuclear-powered, nuclear-armed pride of the Indian Navy. The AI automatically instructed the crew of a Chinese cruiser to fire a supersonic, super-cavitating YJ-18 missile to sink the Indian sub. The automated strike sent the Arihant, with its nuclear reactor, its K-15 and K-4 nuclear-tipped missiles, and its crew of 95 souls, to the bottom of the Bay of Bengal. AI blindsided diplomatic efforts to wind down the crisis.

The direct hit on the PLA encampment struck a raw nerve. All of China instantly united against India's cold-hearted extermination of sleeping soldiers. Demands for justice did not have to be orchestrated or fabricated. Even Col. Singh was outraged, partly because it put him and his troops in mortal danger and partly because he knew the war was nothing more than a political charade being played by stupid politicians, not worth the blood of soldiers, his or theirs. No more singing.

"Well," president Xi said to his inner circle of advisors, "At least we have the people united behind the Party. If we can keep the situation from going nuclear, we can still emerge victorious. We shall freeze all military operations and invite the Indians to do the same."

The sinking of the Arihant ignited -white-hot fury throughout India. Rescue patrols displayed personal items retrieved from the wreckage at sea – a Sikh turban with a navy insignia, shoes, pages from a diary... "Well, this certainly bodes well for the elections," Prime Minister Modi confided to his national security advisor. "The country is more unified than ever before. If we can prevent the situation from going nuclear, we might come out okay. Let's cool things down."

Then, the world as we knew it faded to black when thousands of satellites started crashing into one another, like the mosh pit at a Metallica concert. The Kessler Effect was real.

CHAPTER TEN

The Dark Side of the Moon

It had taken China and Russia two years to build the secret installation on the dark side of the moon, using their International Lunar Research Station (ILRC) as a cover for secret missions to build a moon base equipped with additive manufacturing machines designed to produce killer space drones "like sausages." During the dark days of the Cold War, Soviet premier Khrushchev banged his shoe on the podium at the United Nations as he bragged that the USSR was churning out ballistic missiles "like sausages," but it was a lie. America's secret satellites showed President Eisenhower that there was no missile gap. The drone factory on the moon was no lie.

The Blossom Flower moon base consisted of a simple warehouse structure and separate living quarters for visiting astronauts. Located inside a large crater in the southern polar region, the base was accessible from both nearby Chinese and Russian moon bases via lunar rover vehicles. Chinese and Russian cosmonauts could easily slip away from their main bases to work on the Blossom Flower project under the cover story of conducting scientific studies and mining operations inside the crater. A small modular nuclear reactor provided power for the base and the automated production line that produced the "hornets" -- huangfeng in Mandarin and shershen in Russian.

The cosmonauts brought the aluminum, titanium, nickel-cadmium, and aluminum-beryllium powders that the 3D printing machines used to build the huangfeng by layering row upon row of the alloy powders to produce ready-to-use space drones. The finished units were fitted with thrusters, extendable probe arms, and laser weapons. All they needed were plug-in power packs containing a capsule of plutonium

238 and a shot of propellant, which the visiting cosmonauts added at the end of the production line. Mission control centers in China and Russia sent software instructions directly to the finished murder bots.

The finished satellites were ready to be loaded into the breach of a mile-long mass driver (a large rail gun) hidden inside the crater. The rail gun would shoot each hornet into a westward-facing -sub-orbital trajectory. When they reached apolune, they fired a burst of their thrusters to reach lunar orbit before performing a burn on the dark side of the moon to descend into the desired geosynchronous altitude.

Once in GEO, the hornets used their arc jet propulsion thrusters to maneuver into positions close to their prey and extend their "stinger" probe arm to hook onto their target. The insidious little creatures would maneuver close to a satellite, attach to it like a blood-sucking leech, and download data from their prey's operating systems before infecting them with malicious computer viruses. Once infected, the hollow husks were left to float aimlessly in space.

The plan was for a swarm of Chinese-Russian murder hornets from the Blossom Flower moon base to attack the key nodes of the US Silent Barker space reconnaissance network. These were some of the most sensitive, -highest-priority American military intelligence satellites in GEO. The Blossom Flower swarms would render them deaf, dumb, and blind. How China and Russia knew which secret US satellites were the most vital and vulnerable was a separate question of espionage. Clearly, they had inside information about the most sensitive US systems. But that was a problem for another day.

Blossom Flower targeted the US. But why? Why would Xi and Putin want to expand the sputtering China-India border war by attacking America in space? Why now? Was Xi preparing to attack Taiwan? Was Putin ready to resume Russia's failed aggression against Ukraine? Was this the moment in history when Beijing and Moscow felt confident enough to attempt a killing blow against the American-led, rules-based, liberal, Post-World War Two global order? Were they ready for war with the USA, or calculating that the US was too weak and divided to fight? Was this their plan all along, or did they see an opportunity to take advantage of the India-China crisis?

Xi called Putin in the Kremlin on their secure communication link. Putin had survived multiple assassination plots by Wagner Group hit squads and oligarch cabals. He maintained his iron grip on power through tried-and-true methods forged by Lenin, Stalin, and the KGB, continuing the tradition of mercilessly crushing dissent and immersing the population in an echo chamber of false narratives about Russian greatness. As long as the oligarchs got their cut, they didn't care.

"Vladimir, our time has come. The correlation of forces has aligned with our mutual interests in ushering in a truly multi-polar distribution of global power. It is time to unveil the Blossom Flower. We shall both send scientific missions to our respective moon bases. They will meet at Blossom Flower to initiate the plan."

"I agree with your assessment, Chairman Xi. It is time. It is past time for us to reassert our combined power to end the era of American hegemony. Blossom Flower is just the beginning. We shall fight the NATO Nazis in the West while you fight them in the East. They are weak. Together, we are unstoppable and ready to usher in a new era of peaceful coexistence."

"My dear friend, we are not going to fight the Americans. There is no need. They will defeat themselves. Blossom Flower will consume their attention. Move quietly but quickly against your neighbor and let NATO dither with the space distraction while your forces move swiftly to recover your territory. You will not need your old GLASNOSS navigation system. The special communications gear we provided to you last year will enable you to coordinate your ground, sea, and air operations. Did you not wonder why the Huawei equipment we sold you was so affordable? We will not miss the old space systems. As you restore your historic empire, we shall reclaim our wayward province, Taiwan. Say nothing. Deny everything. Make no statements. Move quickly."

"I'm not sure I understand, comrade Xi. With Blossom Flower or Red Rose, as we call it in Russia, the Americans and their allies will be incapable of a military response. Is this not our moment to vanquish them from the world stage?"

"Trust me, Vladimir. Our territorial objectives will become a fait accompli. The Americans call it a gray zone, but we both know that winning without fighting is the best option. Our information confrontation capabilities will shape the narrative about the new reality, a better, more just world for all. The world is tired of the Americans. With their military forces rendered deaf, dumb, and blind, they will chase their tails for weeks. It will be a done deal, as they say. There will be many meetings, calls, statements, hearings, and proposals, which we will graciously entertain. By the time the Americans figure out what has happened, the new world will have already begun."

"Ahh, I see. Winning without fighting. General Gerasimov used to talk about such things before his unfortunate accident. This is what we call the "red theory of victory," in which we deescalate the conflict by raising the stakes. If we use a tactical nuclear weapon, the Americans will run away like frightened little girls. Blossom Flower will serve this same purpose by knocking them senseless while we snatch the gold from their purse."

"Well, something like that. It's an old Chinese concept. Vladimir, it would be helpful if our friends around the world would join the chorus when we unveil Blossom Flower and usher in the new world order. I have already invited the Pakistanis and North Koreans to chime in with some missile tests and provocative military exercises. You might persuade your Belarusian, Iranian and Syrian friends to join as well. We can both suggest to our African friends how their willingness to make positive statements could benefit them, personally as well as nationally. Do you think your Indian friends might agree to take a neutral stance and call for peace talks at the UN? I suspect Modi is looking for a way out of his predicament, and he is desperate to get a place on the Security Council. Our little skirmishes with them have proved to be quite useful as a misdirection for the main event. We just need the Americans to dither for a bit, to fiddle as Rome burns, as it were. By the time they awaken from their slumber, Ukraine and Taiwan will be reunited with their historic motherlands, and the new world will have begun."

"It is a good plan. I will speak with our revolutionary brothers and sisters. Many have long awaited this moment. The BRICS, Cuba, Iran, Syria, Libya, Venezuela, brother Ortega in Nicaragua, Hezbollah and Hamas, and many others. It will not be hard to persuade them to seize the moment. We will amplify our information campaigns to build support for these historic changes."

"Thank you, Vladimir. It is indeed a historic moment. I am glad we will share it. When the Blossom Flower opens, you know what to do."

Ending the call, Xi turned to his advisors and said, "He's a fool, albeit a useful one. I assume somebody is waiting in the wings to take over when they kill him." Then he gave the order to initiate Blossom Flower.

Within hours, cosmonauts loaded scores of hornets into the rail gun and launched them into lunar orbit, where they dropped into GEO and located their prey. The swarm converged on America's most secret and stealthy intelligence satellites like an army of ants on the carcass of a caterpillar. The hornets enveloped the Silent Barker spy satellites, attached their stinger probe arms, and sucked out their secrets before rendering them useless with short laser bursts. It was done.

"We're under attack!" Once again, it was Col. Yater who heard the screams from space and began shouting orders inside the operations center at Vandenberg Space Force base. "Call the Chairwoman of the Joint Chiefs and tell her to inform the President. We are under attack. We need to go to Def Con One now!"

Ghandi's prediction that "an eye for an eye makes the world blind" was proven correct as the burgeoning, radioactive wall of space junk mowed down satellites like a weed whacker. Now, everyone was truly blind. If the carnage had occurred on a traditional battlefield, it would have qualified as a scorched Earth strategy. This was a scorched sky.

Darkness descended as the roiling avalanche of space junk tore its way through LEO. Gamma radiation from the nuclear blasts incinerated key national security assets in LEO, MEO and GEO. Rivers of energy flowed from LEO, through and around MEO, and into GEO, just as Carissa had predicted. GPS navigation systems disintegrated, disorienting military forces across the globe. How many shipcaptains could use a sextant? Autonomous vehicles stopped dead in their tracks or smashed into nearby obstacles. Self-driving cars littered the roadways, blocking traffic as the world descended into chaos and confusion.

Without the satellites on which the world depended, nearly everything screeched to a halt. Bank transfers froze, instantly crippling commercial transactions around the world. Trains, planes, trucks, and ships stopped in their tracks, immobilized like lost children looking for their mothers. Deliveries of food, oil, gas, chemicals, equipment, building materials, and consumer goods ceased. With no traffic controls, airports, public transit, ports, and freeways throughout the world could not function. Weather forecasts stopped. Emergency services sat idle. Hospitals quit operating when medical records vanished and supplies ran out. Electronic records for everything from law enforcement to credit cards were extinguished. No permits could be issued, no courts to render justice, no marriages or divorces. Prisons across the globe went on lockdown. There were no reservations to be made, no streaming music or movies, no Netflix or YouTube. There was no internet and no social media. The space blackout made the pandemic of 2020 look like a staycation.

Lesser developed regions and nations were less affected by the blackout because they were less dependent on satellite infrastructure than other more "advanced" societies. Traditional ways of doing things had inherent advantages, as older people were fond of reminding younger generations. When you've got nothing, you've got nothing to lose. However, even in developing countries in Africa and Asia, where innovative people had discovered ways to use cell phones to circumvent the need for old-fashioned bureaucratic institutions, the destruction of LEO still ruined lives.

Most cell phones still worked, but without the internet it was not possible to transmit data. And with no data, there was very little business. Where did all the data go when the satellites crashed? Perhaps in the Earth-bound cloud, if it had survived. How much data would be lost? Could it be restored? Would it be destroyed or altered? What would happen to the billions of transactions that were in process when the satellites disappeared? What about the digital records that held the stories of humanity?

A few communications satellites in GEO had escaped the storm that wiped out nearly everything in LEO. A trickle of emergency broadcasting provided essential information, but global media outlets were blinded like everyone else. Without knowing it, the world had become more dependent on space than most people realized.

On her way home from work, Carissa stopped at the ATM to get some cash. The machine was frozen, and the video display read, "We're sorry.

This location is experiencing technical difficulties. We apologize for the inconvenience. Please try again later." Across the street, she noticed a long line at the gas station. The pumps were not working. At the Safeway, the cash registers were not accepting credit or debit cards. "Uh oh," she thought.

CHAPTER ELEVEN

Children of Light and Children of Darkness

American President Keala Kennelly spoke with key U.S. allies before calling the leaders of India, China and Russia. The leaders of Japan, South Korea, Australia, and Canada were all members of the Artemis Accords who had endorsed the updated code of conduct for space operations. Every member of NATO except Turkey and Hungary pledged their full support for a unified effort to stop the space war, clean up the mess, and deter Russia and China from further aggression.

In her call with Prime Minister Modi, the Indian PM requested urgent U.S. military assistance but added the condition that it all must be "made in India."

"Just send us the money and the technology, as you did with Ukraine," he instructed before warning the President that India "would not countenance interference in our rightful and justified defense of Indian sovereignty, wherever it extends."

"Of course, Mr. Prime Minister. We respect India's sovereignty and your right to protect it. The Chinese incursions in the border region are unacceptable, and we applaud your successful efforts along the Line of Actual Control. We welcome India's role as a security provider for the region and as a counter to Chinese aggression. Our bilateral military cooperation is a centerpiece of the emerging global order, and our technology-sharing arrangements are having truly strategic effects. What we are proposing now is to extend the benefits of the US-India partnership to the space domain."

"We shall defend our interests against colonial chauvinism wherever it exists, whether it is in the mountains, at sea, in the cyber world, or the space domain."

The President thanked Modi for "India's endorsement and participation in the Artemis Accords" and heaped praise on "the positive trend of increasing cooperation between the world's largest democracies." She wished Modi luck in his upcoming elections, venting to her NSC staff, "Why does everything have to be so complicated with this guy? We're trying to help him. We like India. At least with Xi and Putin, we know where they stand."

In her next call, the Chinese premier professed no knowledge of the "unusual phenomena affecting the global space commons" and assured the President that the "minor border skirmish" in the mountains would soon have a peaceful outcome. Keala "welcomed the peaceful resolution of the conflict in the Himalayas." Xi then offered China's "preeminent scientific capabilities to assist Washington with any infrastructure difficulties it may encounter" and suggested the formation of an international scientific commission to investigate UFOs, which he suggested might have caused the satellite blackout. He did not, however, share his growing concerns about the rising discontent across China. Xi then offered to sell Huawei electronics to repair broken US infrastructure. "We have excellent and very cost-effective communications equipment available to assist you, should you need it. We are here to help."

President Kennelly thanked the communist leader for his gracious offer and expressed optimism about the prospects for cooperation in solving the world's most urgent problems. "We look forward to working with your experts to correct the problems that are affecting us all. And I trust that during this difficult time, all nations will refrain from precipitous actions that can only serve to exacerbate the situation."

After the call, Kennelly quipped to her White House staff, "At least now he knows that we know what he's up to. Please arrange an NSC principal's meeting. It's time to make our next move. And make sure the nerds from Livermore are invited, including Dr. Moore."

Finally, in her call to Putin, he professed no knowledge of the space wars but took the opportunity to accuse the United States of "wanton acts of aggression intended to re-impose the West's corrupt system of liberal values into the heavens." He professed to know nothing about the space war except that "we are once again the victims of American greed and perfidy" and told her that Russia "would not stand idly by while you extend NATO into space." President Kennelly thanked Putin and assured him that "NATO stands shoulder to shoulder with Ukraine and remains committed to protecting every inch of NATO territory. What goes on inside the borders of Russia is not our concern. However, I want you to understand that preserving the free and fair uses of space is a vital national interest of the United States." Turning to her staff, she said, "What an ass clown. I hope he gets the message. We don't need another deterrence failure."

The President wanted to address the nation on TV but had to settle for radio, which could be quickly restored to reach every American household.

"My fellow Americans, we face a new type of conflict, one that affects all of us in our everyday lives. We are no longer separated from the battlefield. Every one of us is directly involved, regardless of our age, race, or gender. The attacks we are experiencing make us all combatants. Make no mistake; our military remains the strongest in the world and the strongest in space. We shall protect our homeland, our allies, our friends, and our interests throughout the world. This is not in doubt. I will be speaking to you again soon about our military response to these acts of aggression.

But first, I want to talk to you about where we go from here as a nation. Our current difficulties bind us closer together, as we must rely on our neighbors, friends, and family to survive what amounts to an unnatural natural disaster. We are resilient and united as a nation, and we will do what we have always done when faced with adversity. In some ways, we are being forced to return to a simpler way of life, to more basic ways of doing things, the way our parents and grandparents did things before the internet, before cable TV and streaming media, before cell phones, computers, and ATMs, before AI and the Internet of things. Satellites brought us prosperity and will again.

But for now, we know what we must do. We've done it before. If we can't use artificial intelligence, we can rely on good old-fashioned human intelligence. Everything will take longer. We will have to do things in person, face to face, on paper, and closer to home. Many modern conveniences that we have come to rely on have been temporarily removed from our lives. What if we use this as an opportunity to reunite, to get to know each other again, to focus on the things that matter most, and to move our country forward with a renewed commitment to community spirit and national patriotism? What if we give one another the benefit of the doubt, withhold judgment, and reach out to our neighbors? We must learn how to respect our differences. If we do this, we will come out stronger. And I can assure you of two things. First, we shall prevail in this conflict. Second, we shall face it together and find strength in unity. God bless America, and God bless our brave men and women in uniform."

In Beijing, Xi Jinping was starting to have second thoughts. Blossom Flower had blinded the Americans as planned and created the desired opportunity to invade Taiwan, but the ensuing mess had blinded him as well. Losing the internet was one thing, but losing the CCP's national surveillance network, the backbone of its ability to control China's restive provinces and crush opposition movements, presented a different problem. Almost a billion video cameras monitor every public space in China.

They feed their data into an enormous database where facial recognition software matches people with files that contain their addresses, family connections, purchases, medical records, DNA and travel history to assign each person a "social credit" ranking. The system relies on satellites to transfer data. Huawei cell towers alone could not handle the volume. The space war had robbed the CCP of a central pillar of its means of repression just as protests were breaking out across the country. Xi knew that he and the CCP could survive without Alibaba and Tic Toc, but not without their surveillance and control systems. Satellite information was key to his ability to nip protests in the bud before they swept across the country like wildfire. "Those fucking Falun Gong fanatics are just waiting for an opportunity to light the match," he spewed. He needed to get the China-Saudi version of Starlink up and running fast.

Xi still planned to use the crisis to launch his long-contemplated attack on Taiwan and settle that problem once and for all, but domestic tranquility came first. Chaos has its merits but also carries risks. Already, the Ministry of State Security (MSS) was reporting protests in Xinjang, Tibet, and Hong Kong. Factory workers in Shenzhen province, where they churned out everything from iPhones to Christmas ornaments, were demanding higher wages and better working conditions. He didn't care that most of the PLA, the Navy, and the Air Force were bogged down and idle. He never wanted a real war, anyway. "Tell everyone to hold their positions, except those in the East preparing for the great rejuvenation and the liberation of Taiwan. Put them on alert." he barked at his military commanders.

His economic advisors dared not say, "I told you so." As usual, General Jang waited to see which way the wind would blow, wondering how Xi would attempt to turn this potential threat to his power and that of the CCP into a face-saving victory. Xi needed a way out. Would a victory over Taiwan reignite patriotic fervor or unleash hidden dangers?

In India, Modi considered his options. Fight or flight? He, too, contemplated how to turn the war into a political victory. The nuclear tests had been popular. Expressing the Indian leadership's longstanding ambivalence towards its military, he waved off the advice of his military commanders, who claimed to have a relative advantage over the PLA because they relied less heavily on satellite communications than the Chinese or American militaries. "With the PLA stuck with its paws in the honey jar, we are in a position to push their Army beyond the LOC, into the mountains, knock their air force out of our skies, and shove their navy out of the Bay of Bengal. We have them where we want them," advised General Singh. "Sir, the fact that we have not completed the full integration of our forces with our NAVIC space communications systems is a blessing in disguise. We don't rely on the space domain as much as our enemies. Plus, we wisely purchased up-to-date targeting data from Maxar and Planet, the American satellite imagery companies. Remember, in the land of the blind, the one-eyed man is king. Let's teach them a lesson, as you always say."

Modi sneered and dismissed the general with a wave of his hand, shaking his head in a characteristic South Asian head-bob-swivel gesture at the short-sidedness of his military commanders. "Those morons want to fight World War Three. They would use nuclear weapons if I let them. What can we expect from our Pakistani friends? Will they obey their masters in Beijing and throw gas on the fire, or listen to the Americans and stop their yapping?" Modi had other ideas about how to win in the darkness.

In Moscow, Putin's intelligence services flattered him that his plan to protect Russia had outfoxed everyone by taking steps to protect the

Kremlin from just such circumstances. The truth was that he had nothing to do with any such plan, but his advisors knew what he wanted to hear. "Not only are we still able to conduct military operations, but operation Red Rose," as they called Blossom Flower in Russia, "has provided us with several advantages that we are now prepared to exploit. Specifically, Mr. President, with NATO forces in stasis and unable to operate without their space assets, our forces are positioned to take Kiev in a matter of days. The Huawei communications gear from China is working as planned. We are fully mobile."

Putin was encouraged. Xi had told him to launch the invasion. His FSB and GRU intelligence briefers described deep fissures within NATO, especially inside the German government, where NATO demands for two percent of GDP for defense spending evoked strong opposition, and desires for Ukraine to accept Russian terms remained high. French President Le Pen often channeled former President Trump by saying, "There are good people on both sides of the conflict." She could be counted on to resist NATO intervention. Turkey, of course, would play its usual double game, and Hungary's oafish strongman leader was a reliable and useful idiot. Even in the US, they assured Putin, the combination of rabid Trump supporters and taxpayer fatigue was overtaking mainstream support for Ukraine's defense. Now was the time to make their move.

Putin's generals goaded him: "With the Americans and NATO floundering in space, thanks to Red Rose, we are unopposed. We have already prepared the battlespace by infiltrating our covert forces, whom the Americans like to call 'little green men.' They are already meeting with their deep cover assets throughout Ukraine, waiting for our signal to begin sabotage operations and leadership assassinations. Our troops have been replenished with short and long-range munitions, and our logistics and supply lines are strong and reliable. Sir, comrade leader, we are ready. We will retake Crimea as we did before and re-enter Ukraine in a focused pincer movement from Donbas in the east and Belarus to the north. Wagner fighters have been paid and are ready. We will capture Crimea and Kiev in three days. Finally, the Nazi Jew Zelensky will pay for his crimes."

Putin didn't care about the space war, Red Rose, or the South Asia border war. He craved victory over Ukraine as the next step toward rebuilding the Russian empire. With America cut down to size and China on his side, he would restore the global dominance once enjoyed by the former Soviet Union. This was his moment.

CHAPTER TWELVE

Throw a Coat Over It and Smack It With a Hammer

At Space Command headquarters in Colorado, the secret plan to deploy the experimental Claws, known as Op Plan 8080, or Operation Quicksilver, was taking shape. The President had given her approval to implement the scheme devised by Col. Yater at Space Force Base Vandenberg, George Downing at the NRO and the entrepreneur Lucky Slater to deploy a small army of space junk scoopers to clean up the debris polluting the orbital pathways. But first, they had to get the scoopers into orbit, and that was looking more difficult by the minute.

The original Quicksilver plan for the claw was designed to cope with a few collisions that threatened a small number (the number was classified) of critical US space assets. Ten experimental claw satellites (with two in reserve) would be deployed from the Boeing X-37B orbital test vehicle to chase down and neutralize the offending space trash. Once delivered to the polluted areas of LEO, MEO and GEO, the claws would maneuver into the debris fields, matching the speed of the marauding space garbage, and deploy giant umbrella-like magnetic scoopers to corral the debris like cowboys roping cattle. The umbrellas were equipped with directed energy beams to consolidate the debris and then fuse the stray fragments, like a bug zapper on a hot summer night. The remaining "dirt clods" of aggregated space trash could then be tracked and avoided, like small asteroids, and clear the way for safe space operations. That was Carissa's job, to navigate through the debris fields.

Lucky liked to describe the process with an analogy from a scene in the movie Christmas Vacation, where a squirrel hiding in the Christmas tree terrorizes Clark Griswold's (played by Chevy Chase) family. Clark described his plan to neutralize the squirrel: "I'm going to catch it in the coat and smack it with a hammer. It's the same thing with the space junk," Slater explained. "We'll catch the debris with a coat and smash it with a hammer. Only the coat is a force field, and the hammer is a beam of energy." The problem, however, was the sheer scale of the multiple debris fields that had been created carried too much junk for the small number of claw units they had available for the Quicksilver mission. Too many squirrels, not enough jackets, or hammers. One X-37 orbital spaceship and a dozen experimental claw units were not nearly enough. They needed more.

Lucky had a plan, but it went way beyond the classified, compartmented Quicksilver program he was working on with his government colleagues. Lucky's plan would fabricate hundreds of claws and deliver them to the debris fields that were obliterating everyone's satellites. First and foremost, he needed to clear a path to restore America's eyes and ears in space, "to make space great again," he liked to tell people. His plan would make it possible for the US to repopulate its network of vital national security space assets – especially the ISR, SSA, early warning, and navigation systems, and hopefully start to rebuild a more resilient and integrated space architecture. "The whole thing was a kluge anyway. If we had it to do over again, we would never build it like this. Now we have a chance to do it right."

A super-sized claw operation was necessary to restore essential commercial space operations for the global economy. "We're not going back to the stone age, as much as Greenpeace might like it." Lucky was not a Luddite or a liberal. He loved technology. A do-over of the commercial space domain could improve the haphazard cluster of satellites that created the mess in the first place. Plus, and close to his heart, Lucky wanted to revive the dream of space exploration and colonization. He wanted to live on his Malibu space station.

Slater got busy calculating how many claw bots he would need to clean up the heavenly trainwreck. Hundreds? Thousands? "It took us six months to make a dozen for the Space Force mission. We have to do better than that. We need at least a hundred to make a dent in LEO shit." Lucky estimated. No time to lose. He could start making claws at his production facility in Palmdale, where he was building his Malibu space station. They had a few high-end additive manufacturing machines there capable of printing some of the satellites, but it still wasn't enough. Not even close. "Where do I get a hundred precision metal 3D printing machines, like the German EOS? No time to buy and install them. We're going to have to use somebody else's machines. I'm going to need help. Damn." He hated asking for help.

If he could make enough claw bots on the ground, the next problem would be transporting them to space. As he calculated how to transform his plan into reality, he mumbled to his dog, Dora, who listened intently, her head cocked sideways in that quizzical dog gesture that makes people think that dogs understand every word of what they are saying: "That's a shitload of payload and dozens of launches. Space Command will freak out – if I tell them."

Dora lived with Lucky on his boat, a forty-two-foot Beneteau Grand Tourism yacht called the Lucky Dragon, in the Marina del Rey harbor, close to the Los Angeles Space Force Base. A scruffy rescue mutt, he had named her after the iconic Malibu surf legend Miki Dora, but most people assumed she was named after Dora the Explorer, the cartoon character. No matter. Dora went everywhere with Lucky. "The X-37B holds about ten units. There are two of them, plus the 37A prototype, if it still works. That's thirty. Not enough. I wish we had a space shuttle.

Maybe I can steal the Discovery from the Smithsonian. No way around it. I need some SpaceX Falcon 9s."

His plan was taking shape. He would start by making hundreds of claw bots and then deliver them to space. All he needed was an additive manufacturing facility and enough heavy-lift rockets to get the claws into orbit. No problem. He considered using the International Space Station as his manufacturing and distribution hub for the claws but rejected the idea because of the added logistics of shuttling the building materials - mostly aluminum alloys and some polymers - to a space workshop. Same for Malibu. Eventually, he knew it would be possible to mine the materials on the moon and from asteroids and make all kinds of things in space, but not yet. "I'll bet that's what the Chinese and Russians are doing up there, on their secret moon base. They're violating the Outer Space Treaty and screwing up the whole solar system for everyone else. What a bunch of assholes."

In addition to the twelve claw bots that Space Force had ready to stop the attacks on the Silent Barker national security missions in GEO, Lucky figured he would need at least fifty additional claws to clear a path through LEO to make it usable, and another dozen for MEO, which was far less populated and therefore had less junk flying around in it. Once the claw production system was up and running, he could add about a dozen more per week for as long as it took to restore the orbital pathways. "This is it," he told Dora. "You want to go to space, girl? Let's go find Laika."

CHAPTER THIRTEEN

Red Dawn

Carissa's team was furiously reporting the results of their calculations. "It's all gone," she told Yater and the Space Command leadership on a secure conference call. "Think of an avalanche that destroys a village. LEO is like that. A full Kessler wipeout. The avalanche of debris and electromagnetic fields wiped out pretty much everything." They had loaded all of the data into Duke, synched it with Oppie at LANL, and ran the codes by networking the high-performance computers at LLNL, LANL, Sandia, and Oak Ridge National Laboratories. Normally, those computers were reserved for classified computations to keep the US nuclear stockpile safe and reliable, but Rell Sunn and Carissa's team got permission from the lab directors to pool their resources to model what was happening with the debris fields in space. LEO was a total loss, MEO was probably recoverable, and the debris from the attack that reached GEO might be managed.

The good news for Space Command was that Carissa's team had charted a clear path for the original George and Lucky Claw operation to neutralize and remove the remaining Blossom Flower murder hornets. Launching the X-37B and its payload of claw bots would very likely succeed at clearing and even restoring some vital national security assets in GEO if replacements were ready. Carissa had used her controversial thesis findings about the "rivers of energy" to chart a path for the X-37 through the clouds of glowing debris to reach GEO and deploy its payload of orbital sweepers. "We think you're good to go," she told the group on the secure video call. She was glad that her research had proved useful, but she had a nagging sense that there could be more to the story. She had long speculated that the rivers of energy could be manipulated, possibly by lasers. That could be good news.

At Space Command HQ in Colorado, chief of security Lt. Col. Ed Rothman, watching Carissa and her team report their findings on the video call, signaled to one of his security officers and asked, "Is this chick cleared for Op Plan 8080? Check the roster. How the hell does she even know about Quicksilver?"

The news about MEO was also good. With fewer collisions and fewer critical assets, MEO was less polluted than LEO. And since the Chinese-Russian Blossom Flower attacks had focused on Silent Barker satellites in GEO, Carissa's team had been able to model the debris fields to show how it would be possible to navigate through the junk to get to GEO. MEO was not the most urgent problem and maybe a sweet spot for restoring space systems.

The big problem, as Carissa explained to the top US government military, intelligence, and policy leaders on the secure call, was LEO. The GPS was gone and not recoverable. "There's so much junk in LEO that there's no way to put anything else into orbit. All the commercial satellites are dead. It's a total write-off, I'm afraid. I assume you folks are in touch with the commercial space community, explaining to them what's going on. They must be freaking out. They've lost everything. Plus, we're going to need them to help us get back on our feet."

Nervous glances ricocheted around the Space Command war room like a dinging pinball machine. Aware that they were all on camera, representatives from multiple agencies shifted in their seats and tried not to look uncomfortable. Obviously, the commercial space companies knew by now about the blackout and the loss of their satellites, but whose job was it to tell them that there was a war in space that had wiped out everything and crashed the global economy? Whose job was it to call Elon Musk, John Kramer, and the other satellite operators to tell them what had happened, not to mention ask for their help to win the war and restore the peace?

George, dialing into the meeting from NRO headquarters in Northern Virginia, couldn't resist the urge to comment. "You know, that's why we ran that war game out at Livermore, the one where Dr. Moore warned about this exact thing and told us to prepare for it." Carissa rolled her eyes, forgetting for a second that she was on camera and everyone on the video call could see her expressions. "So let me get this straight," George continued. "We knew last year that something like this was possible. We understood how dependent we were on our commercial space assets for our military and our economy, and our intel folks warned us that the Chinese and Russians were planning an attack. Now, we have a global crisis, and we still haven't told the space companies what happened. Am I missing something? I assume Congress has been informed. How long before this leaks and we start the blame game? Oh, wait, let me make a prediction. It's an intelligence failure, like 9-11 and WMD in Iraq, and the Hamas attack on Israel."

"All right, George, you made your point," replied Major General Birdwell, the chief of space operations at Space Force HQ in Colorado. "Let's figure out where we go from here. From what I'm hearing, it looks good for the special program."

Lt. Col. Rothman interrupted abruptly, "Dr. Moore and her team are not cleared for Operation Quicksilver. And frankly, I'm not sure everyone on this call has the appropriate clearances for this discussion. I suggest we end this meeting and reconvene in executive session when we can confirm that everyone is properly cleared." Now, the eye-rolling was impossible to hide.

"Are you serious right now, Rothman? Who the hell let you out of your cage?" raged Col Yater at Vandenberg. "We're in the middle of a fucking crisis, and you're worried about who is cleared for what compartments?

That's bullshit. We need our A Team on this now. That's who's on this call."

"Thank you, Colonel Yater," replied Gen. Birdwell, trying to lower the temperature.

"Have we even talked to our allies?" Yater continued. "I see we have representatives from the State Department and the White House on the call. Can you update us on the diplomatic state of play? Are we at war?"

Stephanie Gilmore, the White House lead for space policy, who had attended the war game at LLNL, addressed the group.

"Thank you, Colonel Yater. Nice to see you again. And thank you all for participating today. President Kennelly spoke this morning with the leaders of our key NATO and allied space partners. They understand the situation and pledged their full support for our combined actions to address the situation. The President informed this group that we are evaluating options and will keep them fully informed. She then spoke with the leaders of China, Russia, and India, who were, in diplomatic parlance, unhelpful.

For the record, you should all understand that we consider the attack on our space assets to be an act of war. As such, we reserve the right to respond at a time and place and in a manner of our choosing. We are taking appropriate steps, including asking Congress for an official declaration of war. However, that is a separate conversation that is underway as we speak. Secretary of Defense O'Neil and the Chairwoman of the Joint Chiefs of Staff are assessing military options. But let there be no doubt, those involved in this attack will regret their actions."

Gilmore continued from the secure conference room in the Old Executive Office Building, directly adjacent to the West Wing, where the National Security Advisor was preparing to meet with the President.

"As you are aware, President Kennelly has authorized Secretary of Defense Peterson to initiate Plan 8080, which has been discussed here today. With respect to further measures, the President will convene a full NSC principals meeting at the White House tomorrow. This meeting will address space issues and the full range of military, economic, intelligence, and diplomatic matters relevant to the current situation. We will let you know who should attend from your organizations. Dr. Moore, President Kennelly would like you to attend."

Col. Rothman interjected, "With all due respect, ma'am, Dr. Moore is not cleared for this level of classification." "Well, sir," Gilmore replied tersely, "she is now." Ending the video link, Gilmore remarked to her staff, "Who's that asshole? Make sure he's not at this meeting tomorrow -- or any meetings at the White House."

The meeting concluded with an intelligence update from the National Intelligence Officer (NIO) for Space, Lisa Owens. Normally, the intel briefer would begin the meeting, but the agenda had gone off the rails. NIO Owens updated the group on the Chinese-Russian Blossom Flower sneak attack, the effects on the ability of US intelligence to monitor events, and the intelligence community assessment of the damage to US command, control and communications (C3). She concluded by endorsing the LLNL-LANL analyses of the debris fields and their calculations regarding the path for Op Plan 8080, Operation Quicksilver. "We assess with high confidence that 8080 can restore critical assets in GEO, even if it doesn't do much to clean up the mess and restore normal operations in LEO. We're going to need a bigger boat for that." Nobody except Rell Sunn caught her reference to the classic line from the movie Jaws, but Lucky was already working on it.

CHAPTER FOURTEEN

Clausewitz in Space

"Nukes in space are different than nukes on the ground," Prime Minister Modi lectured his staff. "Nobody cares about what goes on in space. I call this a win. What are our poll numbers in Gujrat? Is the price of onions holding steady? Are the farmers minding their fields or out stirring up trouble?" As usual, Modi was focused on domestic politics.

In Beijing, Chairman Xi was having second thoughts. His Minister of State Security, Chen Wenwing, reported growing unrest in Xinjiang, Tibet and Hong Kong, with street protests turning violent and CCP offices being burned. The contemplated assault on Taiwan might help rally the people, but the domestic situation was fragile. His police had their hands full. His navy was playing games with the Indian navy in the Bay of Bengal and scattered along the Nine Dash Line. His army was bogged down in the Himalayas and suppressing riots across a vast, unsettled land. His strategic forces were on high alert, and he had already played his Blossom Flower trump card to cow the Americans and hopefully spark a global revolution. It wasn't working. Perhaps now was not the time to go all-in on Taiwan.

Part of Xi's calculus was the Quad – an informal alliance of the US, India, Japan, and Australia, in addition to the strong support of US allies across the INDOPACOM region. Building on the Five Eyes intelligence sharing arrangement, the Quad countered China's testing of the countries of the region to see how far they would tolerate the PRC's claims on their territorial integrity. South Korea voiced its unwavering support for the Quad and made its bases available to the land, sea, and air forces of the Quad countries. Vietnam, Indonesia, the

Philippines, and Malaysia followed suit. Another influential factor in shaping Xi's assessment was AUKUS, the Australia, US, and UK nuclear submarine agreement that provided nuclear-powered attack submarines to Australia. Xi's navy was no match for their combined warfighting power, at least not yet. Rapid deployment of INDOPACOM, Quad, AUKUS, and allied naval forces near Taiwan persuaded Xi that the Americans and her allies were prepared to fight. With his forces spread across multiple fronts, inside China's borders and beyond, perhaps today was not the day. Deterrence held. Xi blinked, but it was too late. The fuse was lit. Civil unrest was about to explode.

In Moscow, Putin's enthusiasm for reinvading Ukraine had not waned, but he, too, was facing a rising tide of internal dissent, especially within the armed forces. The festering rift between the rival factions of his military and intelligence services fueled infighting between competing oligarchs who backed their favorite contenders for power. He wanted to crush them all if he could, but he had no choice but to play the old game of divide and conquer, playing his rivals off one another, as he had for years. Of course, they all wanted to kill Putin, but they were all in the same position. He needed the support of the warring factions if he was going to invade Ukraine and cling to power. Nuclear, chemical, biological, cyber, or space weapons wouldn't help him quell the longstanding battles between the Army, GRU, FSB, SVR, Wagner, and their Kremlin backers. The Russian people had long since given up hope. With the economy in shambles, they focused their attention on survival. There wasn't enough food. They were starving in the dark.

Beyond his borders, NATO was growing stronger and more united by the day. Putin's nuclear threats had only stiffened their resolve, especially frontline states such as Poland, Finland, Sweden, Estonia, Lithuania, and Latvia, who had all offered to host US nuclear weapons and missile defenses on their territory. America's Asian allies pledged their support for NATO, and NATO reciprocated with its support for their defense against Chinese and North Korean aggression. Deterrence, like the Grinch's heart on Christmas, grew three sizes that day.

At the White House, President Kennelly addressed her National Security Council. Carissa had taken the red-eye flight from San Francisco and arrived in time to clear White House security and find her seat in the Situation Room. She sat in the back row between NSC Director Stephanie Gilmore and National Intelligence Officer for Space Lisa Owens, who had attended her wargame in California. The President welcomed her cabinet officials and got down to business.

"We have been attacked. Our instinct is to fight, and we will. However, we need to be clear about our objectives. What are we fighting for? Vengeance is not enough. We are fighting to protect our country, our way of life, and the lives of our allies whom we have pledged to defend. We know Russia and China do not share our values and would attempt to suppress us and our allies if they could. They took their shot, and they failed. We and our allies are standing tall as they confront the restless thirst for freedom from within their borders. We are winning, both militarily and in the battle for hearts and minds.

"We are here today to chart the path forward. I do not believe it is in our interest at this time to respond with military force. Deterrence was tested and held strong. They attacked us in space, where they miscalculated the consequences. I believe we must double down on deterrence for the future. That is what we are here to discuss. I have authorized the implementation of Op Plan 8080, which will begin the process of restoring the space environment that was so dangerously harmed by the reckless actions of China and Russia. I want to hear from you, my trusted advisors, about where we go from here."

Secretary of Defense Jack O'Neil spoke next.

"Madam President, with all due respect, the reason we were attacked was because deterrence failed. We can't just wave a magic wand and pretend that deterrence has been fixed. We need first to restore the balance. The problem is that we have not established deterrence in space, or the cyber domain, for that matter. We need to show China and Russia that aggression in space has consequences. They need to pay a price. They need to fear us."

The Secretary of State, Margo Oberg, weighed in with a diplomatic perspective.

"If I may, we are at an inflection point. The old world is gone, and a new one has not yet formed. With no governance, there are no rules in space. But now, there is an opportunity to establish some real standards of behavior to guide national space policies. We all know what the rules should look like. We drafted the Artemis accords. Perhaps now is the time to negotiate a treaty to guide space development."

"They knew the rules, and they ignored them," Secretary O'Neil snapped.

National Security Advisor Lisa Anderson added:

"It's fine to have a treaty, but how would it be verified and enforced? Are you suggesting a new international organization for extraterrestrial affairs? Laws are worthless without cops and courts."

Secretary State Oberg responded.

"That's what I mean by an inflection point. In my view, the time is right to advance concepts of global governance. The world is reeling from the effects of a 'might makes right' approach. The global economy is in shambles. People are hurting. There is a desire for law and order in space, in the cyber domain, and even for the climate. We've pushed the realist theory to its limits. We need to try something different."

Secretary O'Neil countered.

"What you are proposing has been tried many times before. Multilateral agreements only work when they are backed by military, economic and political power. If you want global governance, it needs to be supported by an enforcer who wields the power to ensure compliance, which always seems to be the United States. I am not opposed to treaties, but I strongly favor the restoration of our integrated deterrence posture as a prerequisite to multilateral diplomacy. We need to reinforce strategic nuclear deterrence and conventional deterrence and devise a strategy for space deterrence. Then, perhaps we can afford to try again to establish global norms."

President Kennelly reacted to the discussion by adding, "I see no reason why we can't do both."

National Security Advisor Anderson asserted, "Job number one is to cool down the current mess and make sure things don't escalate. We need to stop this from getting worse before we can even contemplate making it better."

CIA Director Lakey Peterson updated the group on the latest intelligence reporting. "HUMINT and SIGINT reporting suggests that Xi and Modi are both looking for a way out of their standoff. They don't want to escalate, and both are consumed with paranoia about their domestic political situations. We think both would welcome a peace plan that allowed them to claim victory and go home. We also have reports that Putin is having second thoughts about having another go at Ukraine. Our National Intelligence Officer for Space, Lisa Owens, will update you on our assessment of the space domain."

NIO for Space Owens continued:

"Thank you, Director Peterson. We can confirm with high confidence that the attacks on Silent Barker in GEO were conducted from a secret moon base, code name Moon Flower. The joint China-Russia project built an unknown number of hunter-killer drone bots that attached themselves to our assets and disabled them. We are assessing the potential breach of classified information, but we must assume that Beijing and Moscow succeeded in exfiltrating a large volume of sensitive information from the assets. We assess with medium confidence that the plot was intended as a shock and awe tactic that would freeze the United States and enable Beijing and Moscow to seize the moment to invade Taiwan and Ukraine, respectively. Xi apparently persuaded Putin that American inaction would usher in a new era in world affairs in which China and Russia would replace the US as the predominant powers. The 'escalate to de-escalate' concept is reminiscent of the Gerasimov doctrine, the former Russian defense minister, before his accident, who advocated for quickly raising the stakes in a conflict with the West to cause us to back down. We can also confirm with high confidence the assessment that LEO is completely trashed. That's a technical term."

The Chairwoman of the Joint Chiefs of Staff, Admiral Burleson, reported on the military situation.

"We concur, Madam President, that the current military situation does not pose an immediate threat to the homeland. We have established alternative communications with our forces, and we are able to function without the damaged space assets. We are ready to conduct offensive operations as ordered."

The President turned to face Carissa, seated in a row of chairs lined up against the wall behind the cabinet officials at the table. "Dr. Moore, what do you think about a new set of rules for space?"

Carissa thought about crawling under the table or running for the door but decided against it. There was no escape. The President and her entire cabinet were staring at her. She had to say something.

"Madam President, I'm just a scientist and have no expertise in political matters. This conversation is way beyond my pay grade. If you are asking if I think 8080, Operation Quicksilver, will work, I would say yes. We can restore vital national security satellite functions, especially in GEO. If the idea is to get a fresh start and rebuild the whole space domain, I would say that a more robust effort is required, especially with respect to low Earth orbits. However, I do believe that it would be possible to clear the rubble from LEO and restore the satellite architecture that supports our military and economic interests. What I'm wondering is if we want to open that reconstruction effort to international cooperation. Perhaps we could initiate a Marshall Plan for space to rebuild in a way that most countries would view as advancing their interests."

"Would that include Russia and China? It's their fault that we're in this mess," intoned Secretary of Defense O'Neil.

Carissa replied: "I suppose it would be better to have them inside the tent rather than disrupting things from the outside. I think their scientists would be genuinely interested, even if their leadership is not. Space has been a model of international cooperation for many years – Soyez, the International Space Station, and all the Russian launches of American payloads were successful models of global scientific cooperation. The Chinese are pouring billions into their space program."

National Security Advisor Anderson added, "Russia and China do have significant assets to contribute to a space reconstruction effort. India, as well. Their scientists are first-class. Why don't we at least see if we can get them to help clean up the mess they made?"

Secretary O'Neil parried, "How do we know they won't rebuild their strength and attack us again?"

Secretary Oberg answered, "We don't, Jack. They no doubt will. But as Dr. Moore said, it's better to have them inside the tent where we can see them than stir up trouble outside it. Many countries would welcome a multilateral effort, especially if it gets them free internet. What do we have to lose, especially if we really do reinforce our deterrence posture at the same time?"

President Kennelly summed up. "So how do we do it? We are in violent agreement on the priority of deterrence. Do we have the right forces? Do we need different weapons? What do we need for deterrence in the space domain? Chairwoman Burleson and Sec Def O'Neil, I would like a summary of top priorities for integrated, cross-domain deterrence on my desk by the end of the week. Secretary Oberg, I need a backgrounder on your ideas for a new space treaty based on the Artemis Accords. Have Ambassador Marks in Geneva take the lead on it. End of the week, OK? Next, the clean-up is underway, but it will not be sufficient. What do we need for an expanded remediation of LEO and MEO? Do I understand correctly that GEO is in pretty good shape? Dr. Moore, I want a report from you laying out what we need to rebuild the space domain also by the end of the week."

Carissa was dumbstruck. Since when does the President of the United States tell me what to do? "This is crazy."

"Yes, Madam President. We should also include the private sector if that's okay. That was a big lesson from our war game. We need them to be part of the solution."

"Yes, of course. That's a good point." Turning to her staff, the President said, "Let's plan a meeting for next week with commercial space leaders, including NASA, DOD, Space Command, and the Commerce Department. I suppose we have to invite Elon and Phil. They are both such a pain in the ass. Make sure they all have the right clearances to discuss what happened and our capabilities to deal with it. We need them to help rebuild the orbital domains. Anything else? Ok, thanks, everyone."

As the meeting ended and the cabinet officials and their staff collected their papers and shuffled their way to the door, President Kennelly looked at Carissa.

"Is it true that you are an Orioles fan?"

"Yes, Madam President. I grew up in Baltimore. My dad worked for the team."

"Please, call me Keala. Any interest in catching a Nationals game?"

"I guess so, yes. Thank you." Carissa thought to herself, "Is she hitting on me?"

The emergency satellite blackout turned out to be a relatively peaceful time across America and the world, sort of like the COVID-19 pandemic of 2020. Life slowed down. The global economy suffered, but local economies met the demand for the essentials of life. Global supply chains shriveled, and big box stores ran out of merchandise produced by cheap overseas labor, but locally-made goods and mom-and-pop stores filled the need. The power came back on. Freeway traffic thinned. Air traffic slowed to a trickle. Air quality improved. It was a time of quiet, inward focus. There were not as many choices, not as many places to go, and not enough of everything, but there was enough to go around. Without the internet and streaming media, people sought entertainment at local theaters, bars and restaurants. America looked a bit more like Europe, with families taking evening walks to greet their neighbors.

Communities banded together out of necessity and muddled through the inconveniences of daily life, as the President had urged in her speech. Around the world, conflicts eased, except in China and Russia where social unrest was reaching the boiling point. Commerce slowed to a trickle, and politics took a break as if God had hit the pause button.

If the only thing that could unify the world was an alien invasion, the satellite blackout came close.

CHAPTER FIFTEEN

We're Going to Need
A Bigger Boat

Lucky wasn't screwing around. He got his 3D printers in Palmdale busy making clean-up claws and called his colleagues to ask for more printers. First, he called his friend Ed Aikau at the classified production facility in Kansas City to ask if they would be able to make a dozen or more Claw bots a month. The Kansas City plant had a long history of making classified parts for secret government projects and had pioneered the production of nuclear weapons parts using 3D printing. "Eddie, old buddy, old pal, I need you to do something for humanity. I need you to make a bunch more of the things you made for Operation Quicksilver."

"Who's the sponsor, Lucky? You know we can't make stuff without a government contract. We need authorization from the USG sponsor."

"What if I can't tell you? I promise that you will get paid. But it's an emergency, and we don't have time for all the usual bullshit of the procurement process."

"Can't you get SOFWERX or AFWERX or DIU to sponsor it? They have authorization to take shortcuts. What about DARPA or your spooky space buddies at NRO? Nobody ever knows what they're up to."

"I need it now, Ed. I needed it yesterday. You could print these things out, no problem. You already have the metal powders. I'll send you the blueprints. It's almost exactly like the other ones from Quicksilver, with a few improvements."

"You know I can't do that, Lucky. We're not even supposed to be talking about that program. Don't you have people in the private sector? What about SpecTech? They do that kind of off-the-books spooky shit, no questions asked."

"Maybe. Thanks for nothing, Ed. Talk to you later."

SpecTech was a contractor that produced specialized equipment for covert operations. Their clients were normally the CIA and black ops SOF units. Lately they had been branching into the space domain with small satellites and covert communications gear. Lucky had worked with them on projects where the demand for a small number of specialized items for a specific operation was not enough to warrant a full production line, which meant they would never be profitable. Lucky found ways to make the special widgets profitable by finding other buyers or designing equipment that used enough of the specialized items to make them profitable. Perhaps, he thought, he could get SpecTech to use their 3D printers to make more of the clean-up claw bots. SpecTech agreed on the condition that it get paid in advance, in cash. Lucky agreed.

His next problem was to find the launch services he needed to deliver the expanded clean-up units to space. He called Yater. "Reny, I can restore the space domain in a few weeks. All I need is ten launches."

"Lucky, I don't know what the hell you're up to, but don't do it. Cease. This is not your call. You could get in a lot of trouble. I'm serious."

Even if he could make the bots and find launch services, Lucky would also need to chart the path into safe orbits amongst the junk in LEO and release the clean-up claws in the exact right places to catch the space trash and bundle it. For that, he called Carissa. "Carissa, I need your help."

"What now, Lucky?"

"I need you and your team to chart a path through all the shit and get us into LEO. We need access to the SPCACECOM tracking units. They are the only ones that have sensors left up there. How about Clark and Hamilton? Are they still up and running? We need a safe passage to deploy the clean-up bots we're making."

"You mean like an expanded Quicksilver? Does Yater and SPACECOM know about it?"

"It's the only way, Carissa. SPACECOM is still shell-shocked. It'll take them weeks to figure out what to do. They're still dicking around with Quicksilver. I'll tell Yater when we have a solution figured out and we're ready to go. We need to get going on this now. We can't wait. All I'm asking you to do is run some calculations on Duke."

"I'll have to ask the team. I can't do it alone. I'll get back to you."

Carissa called her SSA team together to discuss Lucky's plan.

"Our job is to model and simulate orbital collisions. We do that to protect US national security by helping SPACECOM and other agencies to avoid collisions. As you know, the recent collisions have endangered the assets we are supposed to protect, thereby putting our national security at risk. We will be an important piece of the puzzle to restore our space enterprise. We have an opportunity to start that process. However, the US government is still deciding what to do. The question I have for you all is, do we want to jump-start that process and help with the rebuilding process or sit back and wait for orders? I was at the White House. I spoke with the President. I know she wants to get started ASAP, but the US government is not capable of moving quickly, even if they want to. We have an opportunity to work with a fast-moving team to expand the clean-up effort, starting in LEO. But, the official orders have not made it through the bureaucracy. There is no funding yet. If we start calculating pathways for the clean-up effort, we risk being accused of taking unauthorized actions and could be held accountable for anything that goes wrong. We would also have to use funding from other projects, which could get us all in big trouble, especially me as your boss. We need to decide as a team whether to do this or not."

"Team America! Fuck yeah!" Rell growled. "Count me in," Garrett McNamara sneered. "Nobody can do a damn thing until we've characterized the debris fields. We can't just sit here with our thumbs up our asses waiting for some bureaucrat to tell us that we're violating safety or environmental regulations. Fuck it. Let's get cranking on this." The team agreed, including Eileen, the intern.

What most of the team did not know was that Eileen, the intern, was a Chinese spy. A year before entering her graduate engineering program at Berkeley, she was arrested at a pro-democracy protest near her home in Hong Kong and given a choice by the Ministry of State Security: Either go to school in America and work for them, or spend her life in prison. She made the obvious choice. Now, she was sending reports about Carissa and her team at Livermore National Lab back to her MSS handlers. She described the big war game, Duke and Opie's computational capabilities, the US space surveillance system, their actions throughout the crisis, Quicksilver, and Rell's tales about a secret program to analyze captured alien spacecraft. The MSS considered Eileen to be a tier-one asset whose reports were read eagerly by top CCP leaders, including Xi himself.

She felt bad about it and told herself she wasn't doing any harm, despite feeling guilty about spying on her colleagues, who she really liked and admired. In another life, she would have liked to join Carissa's team. But she was stuck. If she refused to cooperate, the MSS would round her up and throw her in jail. Her case officer in Hong Kong warned her that the MSS had a network of agents throughout the US who could snatch her in California and transport her back to the PRC at any moment. All she had to do was use the burner phone they gave her to text reports on what she saw at Livermore. Now she had to report on Carissa's trip to the White House, the expedited Quicksilver clean-up plan, and Rell's latest information about alien "biologics." Her reports went straight to the CCP leadership, who were themselves trying to figure out how to regain the advantage in the space domain.

What Eileen did not know was that the FBI tracks sensitive country foreign nationals at the Lab, especially scientists from the PRC. They had connected the phone number she was texting to with the Ministry of State Security. But instead of arresting her, they elected to monitor her to gain insights into the Chinese spy network. Counterintelligence officers had informed Carissa and asked her to play along as if nothing was wrong.

Andrei called her at home.

"Carissa, we need to talk."

"Andrei, I'm really busy. Can we talk next week?"

"I'm sorry. It's not about us. Well, it is sort of about us, but much is happening. You won't like it, but please listen. My institute in Russia, the All Russia Institute of Physics, answers to the government. We don't like it, but our research funding comes from the government, and we have no choice but to make them happy.

"Andrei, I can't help you with funding. I told you that before."

"No, no. Carissa, please listen. I don't need funding. I have funding, but I had to agree to tell them about you, your work at the lab, and us."

"Are you serious? You're spying on me? Oh my god, Andrei. I thought we were friends. Holy shit! Is this a joke?"

"We are friends, and I didn't want to do it, but I had no choice. I would lose my job. But what I wanted to tell you is this: I want to defect to

America. I will tell you everything about our research, things I have not told you. We have studied your research, Carissa. You were right about the rivers in space. The energy flows are amazing. We might even be able to use them to remove space debris. I need to tell you about it. It might help us fix the mess in space."

"Andrei. Why now? What the hell? What am I supposed to do?"

"Tell your bosses. Tell the FBI. Tell your security office at the lab. Tell them I can help."

"Jesus, Andrei. You really put me in a bad spot, especially now. Let me talk to some people and get back to you. Are you hiding? Where can I contact you?"

"Use this phone. It's a burner. Do not call my home. Do not call my work."

"Why? What else am I going to find out? That you're married? That you're insane?"

"That is not funny, Carissa. You know I love only you."

Carissa hung up and took a big gulp of chardonnay. "This can't be happening. What is wrong with these men?"

Lucky was making progress on the 3D printers and focused on getting them to space. He had concluded that he needed at least ten launches to get the first one hundred custom clean-up bots into LEO. He knew SPACECOM had already laid claim to all available launch services for the next few years at least, so there was only one solution. He would have to hijack a few reusable Falcon 9 rockets from their launch pads at Vandenberg and Cape Canaveral. He would load the bots on the hijacked rockets and deliver them to LEO without permission from SPACECOM or SpaceX. He would need insiders in both places, and he had a few ideas about who to ask.

Lucky and Carissa, however, were not alone in thinking about ways to clean up the mess and fix space. Something needed to be done. In India, the Indian Space Research Organization (ISRO) was doing damage assessments on their space program, including their moon bases. The Russians were thinking about how to restore their military and intelligence capabilities, based in part on Carissa's research, as reported by Andrei, and had come up with some novel theories about space-clearing possibilities. Chinese scientists were worried about their moon bases and were busy calculating ways to repopulate their commercial and military networks. Throughout Europe and Asia, space-faring nations and the commercial operators of satellites were already hard at work figuring out how to heal the scorched skies.

CHAPTER SIXTEEN

Quicksilver Messenger Service

With the President's approval, SPACECOM executed Op Plan 8080, Operation Quicksilver. The loadmasters put a dozen Claw bots into the cargo bay of the X-37B experimental spacecraft, and SPACEFORCE launched the spaceplane and its crew on an Atlas 5 rocket from the Kennedy Space Center on a glimmering Florida morning. Following a course selected by Carissa's team to avoid roving bands of space junk, the mysterious unmanned craft navigated through LEO, past MEO, to reach GEO, 22,000 miles from Earth. Once the X-37B reached the vicinity of the damaged Silent Barker reconnaissance satellites, it disgorged its dutiful robot crew from the cargo bay. The Claws used their propulsion thrusters to zoom over to their assigned debris zones and locate any surviving pieces of the precious NRO satellites. The Claws also looked for chunks of the Flower Blossom murder hornets to recover evidence for analysis.

From the control room at Vandenberg, Col. Yater and Lucky Slater monitored the progress of their bold plan. Slater had driven his prototype Tesla truck up Highway 101 from LA, boarded his dog Dora in Santa Maria, and joined the watch party at the Space Force base. Yater lived nearby in Lompoc, but his wife often complained that he actually lived at the base and only visited home occasionally. George Downing, who brainstormed the Claw idea in the first place, monitored the operation from NRO headquarters in Chantilly, Virginia. Carissa and her team, whom the White House had cleared for access to Quicksilver, watched from their op center at Livermore. The SPACECOM commander and his team oversaw the operation from their headquarters at Schreiver Space Force Base in Colorado. Everyone watched in wonder as the Claw bots emerged gracefully from the X-37B, unfolded their antennae, extended their claw arms, and gently motored into space like butterflies emerging from their cocoons and taking flight.

As they approached their designated areas and identified target objects, the Claws maneuvered close enough for visual identification and carefully engaged the wayward remnants. Claw number 8 closed distance on the lifeless husk of what the mission experts watching the video feed identified as one of the top-secret Silent Barker satellites. The Claw moved with short bursts from its thrusters to within ten feet of the burned and bedraggled satellite and extended its claw arm as if to offer a hand to a wounded comrade. The Claw reeled in the damaged satellite and secured it to its luggage rack. Nearby, an unfamiliar object floated helplessly. With a woof of its little jets, Claw number 8 approached the extinguished murder hornet and latched onto it with its gentle hook arm, clasped it to its luggage rack, and returned to the X-37B. Maneuvering close to the mother ship, Claw 8 aligned itself with the cargo bay and eased into its assigned rack.

The additional space taken up by the recovered satellites meant that the X-37B would have to shuttle back and forth several times to recover all the Claws and their quarry. Hearing about the need to make multiple trips, the SPACECOM commander turned to his staff and said, incredulously, "Remind me why we only have one of these? Didn't we figure out a long time ago that we would have to do maintenance on our satellites? Wasn't that the whole idea behind the space shuttle?"

The other Claws located and secured the other Silent Barker satellites and their Chinese-Russian assassins, which were stashed inside the X-37B and repatriated to Earth. The first load landed back at Vandenberg, where NRO and Space Force experts took the classified Silent Barker satellites to a special facility located on the base. Crews removed the

Blossom Flower murder hornets and took them to a separate secure warehouse where teams of NAISC, CIA, DIA, DARPA and national lab experts would analyze them. Rell Sunn couldn't resist turning to Eileen and whispering, "They are taking them to the secret bunker where they keep the alien biologics."

Space Force crews prepared the X-37B to pick up a second load. Lucky was conflicted. "Should I tell Yater about my plan for LEO?" With the X-37B tied up with Quicksilver, he was plotting how to commandeer the launch services he needed for his mega-Quicksilver operation. Let me scope it out first, he thought.

"Reny, this is taking forever. At this rate, it'll take weeks to clear the key orbits in GEO. God knows how long it will take to get the new stuff built and back up there. Months, maybe years. And that's just to restore the Space Surveillance Network. There's so much more to do. We should talk about an expanded plan for LEO."

"The President is way ahead of you. She's already asked us and the private companies to come up with a plan. Carissa is in the middle of it. I don't know why they picked her, but she's got the pen for the plan to fix LEO. We're already talking to the launch services."

Lucky knew this meant there would be little room left for the launches he needed for his plan.

"But the clean-up job is immense, and nothing can happen until we sweep up the mess. One X-37B ain't going to cut it, bro."

"Hey, talk to Carissa. She's best buddies with the President. My priority is to execute Quicksilver and make sure the Chinese and Russians don't try to take advantage of the situation to attack us again. The President does not want to retaliate unless it's necessary to protect the homeland. Job numero uno is to execute Quicksilver so we can restore a temporary replacement for military navigation, communications and ISR platforms. Our forces need to be ready to fight, although it looks like things are calming down. Your contractors are going to get rich from this, as usual. Have you talked to your buddy Elon? Is he ready to hire me at SpaceX?"

"Elon is psycho. Not as bad as Kramer, but certifiably nuts. Everybody knows that. I guess Starlink is trashed, but he's already working on the replacement, building lots of reusable Falcons and Dragons and tons of cube sats. Do you really want to work for that guy? He's crazy. I'm serious, Yater."

"I'm serious about making enough money to send my kids to college. The oldest has her sights set on Harvard or Stanford. She's really smart. I'm just thinking about post-retirement options. I'm getting close. When you put in your retirement papers and start the transition to civilian life, the Skill Bridge program sets you up with prospective employers. I would be free labor for about a year. I hear Elon likes to save money. Could you talk to him? "

"Don't say I didn't warn you, bro. You'd be better off working with me. Not for me, with me. We could clean up LEO and do it fast. Then we could repopulate it with a better architecture that can't be hacked or fucked with. I'm serious."

"Oh yeah? You and what army? How are we going to do all that?"

"Dude, I have an idea."

Quicksilver was a home run. The Claws recovered most of the Silent Barker space surveillance satellites and enough of the murder hornets to confirm where they came from. The intel analysts pieced together the whole story of the secret Russia-China moon base and the Blossom Flower/Red Rose plan to blind America as part of their plan to attack their neighbors, Taiwan and Ukraine. One unwelcome and embarrassing discovery from the forensics was the extensive reliance on

American technologies, including the chips and electronics, without which Beijing and Moscow could not have launched their elaborate assault on America's eyes in the sky. Other parts came from American allies in Europe and Asia. The murder hornets were multinational creatures.

Americans were outraged to discover that so many American companies had contributed to the surprise attack. Congress called the CEOs of big tech companies on the carpet to explain how and why they were helping to arm our adversaries. John Kramer's satellite company, Global Contact, had been instrumental in facilitating surveillance of sensitive US national security sites, targeting US and allied forces, as well as broadcasting a steady stream of anti-American, pro-Russian and Chinese disinformation.

Testifying before the Senate Committee on Oversight and Investigations, Kramer was unapologetic. He lectured the senators about how he was no more responsible for how his customers used his platforms than the gas and electric companies were for how their customers used their services.

When reminded that gas and electric utilities were found to be legally responsible for the widespread death and destruction caused by their unsafe business practices, Kramer launched into a self-righteous rant about how he and his fellow tech billionaire buddies embodied the "pioneering spirit of exploration, willing to risk it all for a chance to the new gaze upon the next frontier." He warned the elected officials that "creeping socialism and government red tape" was a bigger threat than any military conflict.

"I didn't start the war that destroyed my satellites. Governments did. Until they were destroyed, my global technology partnerships were doing more to bring peace than all your tanks and aircraft carriers combined. You should be thanking me, not investigating me."

A senator asked Kramer, "Am I to understand that you see no problem at all with aiding and abetting the enemy who attacked us and that you would do it all over again?" Kramer replied, "Senator, you do not understand how the world works. Governments do not control global economics. The way I see it, this is what happens when governments intervene in the private sector. We had no beef with China or Russia. Governments should stay out of our business."

Kramer's remarks inspired the Committee to draft legislation to impose tighter controls over technology exports to China and Russia, especially chips and microelectronics.

Quicksilver was a success, but it was not nearly enough to clear the debris. The White House meeting with the commercial space leaders illuminated the problem. Even an expanded Quicksilver program would take months or years to clear LEO. Trying to put a positive spin on the situation, US government officials urged their private sector partners to help design a re-imagined, upgraded, "new and improved" space domain. They described special contracting authorities that would reduce red tape and incentivize innovation. They promised expedited funding and liability waivers. The government understood that it needed the private sector, but it was not clear that the private sector believed that it needed the government. At the President's request, Carissa attended the meeting in the Old Executive Office Building. She came away from it, shaking her head. She needed to talk to Lucky about money and business.

Following up on the President's request for a diplomatic strategy, Ambassador Marks delivered her report on the State Department's plans for a new era of global space governance. Starting with the Artemis Accords and the idea that "space unites humanity," a new space treaty would herald the arrival of an era of peaceful cooperation, transparency, interoperability, and communication.

"The draft treaty would be negotiated around these concepts, keeping it simple, like the Nonproliferation Treaty, which has only ten articles. We would stress the offer of assistance in the peaceful uses of space in exchange for pledges not to apply such assistance to military applications. That will provide incentives for developing countries to join. We might want to propose a new space station like the ISS for the new organization to operate, or their satellite network, like Starlink."

Ambassador Marks, the former SEAL, continued with her report:

"We propose to use the clean-up effort to begin the implementation of the treaty. Specifically, the new agency would be empowered to manage, track, and dispose of orbital debris. We must do this anyway so we can make a virtue of a necessity. We would start by engaging with Russia, China, India, and key allies in NATO and Asia to execute the clean-up of LEO under the banner of global cooperation. To get the ball rolling, of course, would require us to pay the lion's share of the costs, at least initially. We would apply the current funding formula for the United Nations, the International Atomic Energy Agency (IAEA), and other UN organizations, where we provide about 25% of the budget. We can also make voluntary contributions to specific activities, as we do with the IAEA safeguards budget. We estimate the cost of a new, multilateral organization for space governance to be in the range of a billion dollars, which brings our initial share to about $250 million.

To save time and money, we would base the new organization either at the Conference on Disarmament in Geneva or at the UN Center in Vienna. Those places are not optimal, but we don't want a new organization to go the way of the Olympics and be located in Beijing or Moscow – or Caracas. Better the devil we know. There is also the possibility of offering to locate it in India."

"Thank you, Caroline," said the President. "What is your timeframe for drafting and introducing the treaty?" "We can have the draft ready in a few weeks, submit it for interagency review and introduce it at the next session of the UN or the CD in the Fall."

The CEOs of the big space companies warned the President that they were already working at full capacity to restore satellite infrastructure without the government. Any plans the government had about building and launching new satellites would have to compete with the burgeoning demand from the private sector, which was not waiting around for guidance. They were already meeting the demand to get new systems into LEO, MEO and GEO. They shared with the group the increasing interest in VLOW, even the Stratosphere. The orbits would be repopulated before the government could issue their requests for expressions of interest or bids for government contracts. Other governments were moving fast as well. The CEOs warned that if the USG had big plans to rebuild the space domain, it had better get moving. John Kramer was already in negotiations with a big China-Saudi group, and Elon Musk, Jeff Bezos, and Richard Branson weren't waiting for permission from anyone.

Carissa came away from this meeting with the same sense of bemusement that she had after the meeting with the private space companies. "Can you just create new treaties like that?" she thought to herself. But those thoughts gave way to more immediate concerns. She had a ball game to get to. The Nationals were playing the Orioles in a regional cross-league match-up, and she had to meet the President at the ballpark.

CHAPTER SEVENTEEN

Lucky's Covert Action

Lucky wondered, who could he trust to steal a rocket? He called Yater.

"Dude, do you really want to work at SpaceX?"

"Yeah, man, I'm ready to put in my papers. I called Skill Bridge, and they're good with me doing my retirement transition at SpaceX. Can you make it happen? I would be forever grateful."

"Yeah, Reny, it can happen. But here's the deal. I need you to secure access to a couple of Falcon 9s."

"Sure, I guess. I mean, it depends on my role there. Right? If I'm scheduling launches, why not?"

"Well, it's part of the plan we talked about to fix space. We need a bunch of heavy lift to get more clean-up bots into LEO."

"What clean up bots? We're using all the Quicksilver bots we have for 8080 in GEO."

"I'm making more, dude. A lot more. Enough to clean up LEO. It's a secret plan to get us back up there. Are you in?"

"I guess, yeah. What's it called, your plan?"

"I don't know. Golden Shower?"

"Not funny. Too weird. How about Silver Surfer? You surf, right?"

"That's fucking awesome, man. That's it. Silver Surfer. I'll get back to you with details. I have a few more calls to make, but get ready for your first day in crazy town with Elon. It's all set."

Next, he called Carissa. What Lucky didn't know yet was that Carissa's relationship with the President had grown into one of real trust and confidence. "Carissa," he urged, "We need to move faster to clean up the space mess. Quicksilver is not even close to what we need. Remember what I told you about? It needs to happen now."

"I hear you, Lucky." Recalling the White House meetings with the private sector and the diplomats, Carissa was worried that it would take years to clean up LEO and repopulate it with a better, more robust and reliable satellite architecture. She was not encouraged by what she had heard from the CEOs, SPACECOM, or the diplomats, although she admired them all. She thought the President probably shared her concerns.

"What's the plan, Lucky? I told the team that you have something cooking. They want to help."

"Your part is to chart the trajectories, lead us through the debris fields like you did with Quicksilver, and find places to put the trash where it won't cause problems. Maybe deorbit some of the big stuff and send other stuff out beyond GEO. You guys are the traffic cops, putting us in the right places and making sure we avoid collisions. Same as you always do, with Duke and Oppie. Do you think we need special arrangements for the electromagnetic pulses?"

"Yes, it's really hot in places, although it's dissipating. But I keep going back to the river idea that you guys all laugh at. The rivers might help, but they might mess things up as well. We're doing some calculations. Lopez at Los Alamos is running the numbers on Oppie."

"OK, baby. Let's go. This is our moment in history. We can do something really good for the world."

"Sure. Whatever. We can do our part. We have some ideas about the reconstruction effort as well. Cube sats, distributed networks, improved optics, anti-hacking, a bunch of stuff."

"Great. We're calling it Operation Silver Surfer. Me, Yater and the Space Force guys are all surfers. Cool, right?"

"Yeah, cool, I guess. Talk to you later."

"OK, baby?" she thought to herself. "What is wrong with these men?"

CHAPTER EIGHTEEN

Girl Power

Carissa met the President at Nationals Park, the slick new stadium built near the old Navy Yard on the Anacostia River. The Nationals filled the hole left when the Washington Senators left DC in 1960 to become the Texas Rangers. Baseball returned to DC in 2006 when they lured the Expos away from Montreal and built the stadium to anchor the redevelopment of the run-down waterfront area. Carissa knew all about it from her dad, who thought it was only right for DC to have a big-league team. For years, the Orioles had benefited from baseball-starved citizens of the nation's Capitol making the trek up Interstate 95 or the Baltimore-Washington Parkway to Baltimore's beautiful downtown Camden Yards Stadium. Now, DC has its showcase stadium and a solidly mediocre team.

Upon arrival at the gate, men and women in dark suits with earpieces whisked Carissa to the President's suite, where President Kennelly was sitting alone with a beer, munching on peanuts. She threw the shells on the ground and said, "Hey, I'm glad you came, Carissa. You want a beer?" "Yes, I'd love one. Thank you." "They're in the fridge over there. There's good stuff and the usual. I'm a Budweiser girl myself. There's also White Claws if you're into that. The food is over there, nothing fancy, just hot dogs and pretzels. Sit here." Carissa grabbed a DC Brau Armageddon IPA and a warm pretzel with mustard and sat next to the President. The teams were still warming up on the field. "Do you think it's weird that I invited you here?" the President said, looking directly at Carissa. "No, madam President, it's just a little unusual for me, that's all."

"I get it. It's weird, I know. But I need a friend, Carissa. I need somebody to talk to about this space stuff, and you've been really helpful. And don't call me madam President. Call me Keala."

"Ok, Keala."

"Carissa, I need to get your perspective on a few things. The CEOs and the diplomats are full of shit. You were there. And my science advisors are such nerds. Where do they get these people?"

"To be honest, I'm one of them, a nerd. The labs are full of them. It's who we are. We love science the way you love politics."

"Fair enough. But you're different. What do you think of our plans to clean up space and repopulate it with a new architecture of satellites? Can they do it, the CEOs and the government?"

"Sure, but it's going to take a long time. Too long. Quicksilver is just a drop in the bucket. We need much, much more than that. More of everything."

"What about the new space treaty? Do you think it's possible to start a new era of peace and cooperation based on the Artemis Protocols?"

"Well, that's really not my area of expertise. The diplomats seem to think it's possible. But I guess I'm wondering why it would work now when it didn't work before. They, Russia and China, knew the rules and did it anyway. What has changed? Plus, we can't even get the world to cooperate on climate change or biological weapons. It's a fine idea, but maybe a bit unrealistic."

"Thank you for your honesty. That's what I was hoping for. We need more than treaties. What about the Nationals? Do you think they stand a chance this year? The pitching is good. Our bullpen is decent. What do you think?"

"Keala, if you want my honest opinion, the Nationals suck. You have one of the worst away-game records in the league, the scoring with men on base is the third worst in baseball, and the team batting average is 221. The pitching is okay, but isn't their combined earned run average close to seven? There's no way. It's a dumpster fire. Sorry."

"Well, that's harsh but true. How about the Orioles? They're looking pretty good this year."

"Yes, the team is really coming together at the right time. We have all the pieces – hitting, pitching, defense. I wish my dad was here to see it. We haven't been this good in a long time."

"Your dad worked for the Orioles, right?"

"Yeah, he was the equipment manager and clubbie for a long time. He took me to the ballpark all the time. It was great. I got to meet Frank Robinson. And Cal Ripken."

"That's awesome. I'm jealous. What do we need to do to fix the space situation?"

"We need something like a super-sized Quicksilver. More of everything – clean-up bots, space launch capacity, and international cooperation. And we need to deter them from attacking us in space. They need to be afraid to do something like this again."

"Do you think I should have retaliated against the Chinese and Russians? What a bunch of lying assholes, Xi and Putin."

"I don't know Keala. They thought they could get away with it, and they kind of did. The reason we have nuclear weapons is not to fight with them but to make it clear to the assholes that the price of doing shit like that is way too high. I'm sorry for the crude language. We need something like that for space. Treaties are fine, but they're just words on paper if consequences don't back them."

"You are a wise woman, Carissa. You want to be in charge of our space policy?"

"I don't understand what you mean."

"I want you to be my science advisor and to oversee this whole space reconstruction and deterrence effort."

"I don't think I'm qualified for that, Madam President, I mean Keala. I'm just a scientist."

"Let me tell you a secret. You're more qualified than most of the swinging dicks who are running the world, acting like they are in charge. I was a CEO and a governor before becoming President. At every step along the way, people told me I wasn't qualified, even when the men doing the job were less qualified than me. You're qualified, Carissa. Believe me. You're qualified."

"I need to be honest with you. There is a plan to fix space, but it's not an official government plan. It's a bunch of space scientists and entrepreneurs. And spies. There are spies from China and Russia trying to help."

"Will it work, this unauthorized plan?"

"Maybe. Yeah, I think it could work."

"What if we made it a secret program, authorized by the President, with you in charge? Would that work?"

"Maybe."

"What about the spies? Will they jeopardize the operation?"

"No, actually. One is our intern, who is telling the Chinese about what we are doing. They might want to help for their reasons. The other is a former lover of mine who is a researcher at a Russian institute who has been stealing my research and conducting experiments to see if I was right. Turns out I was right. He wants to defect and help us use the research to clean up the orbits. Both could be helpful. We might get the Russians to help."

"I told you, you're qualified. Former lover? A man, did you say, if you don't mind me asking?"

"A guy from grad school. A total nerd."

"Well, you can't blame a girl for trying, if you know what I mean. I do want you as my science advisor. And this secret operation is a go. Keep me informed. Lisa Anderson, my National Security Advisor, will be your point of contact. She will bring CIA Director Peterson up to speed. I'll also give you my direct line. Call me any time. The game is starting, and the Nats are going to kick your ass today. You want another beer?"

CHAPTER NINETEEN

With a Little Help from My Friends

Colonel Yater submitted his retirement papers and reported to SpaceX headquarters in Hawthorn, California, close to the LA Space Force Base and Lucky Slater's boat in the Marina del Rey harbor. The Skill Bridge program was designed to help members of the military transition to civilian life by matching the skills they learned in the military with civilian jobs. Yater was a good fit for SpaceX. He would start by shadowing SpaceX managers in various positions to give him a feel for the company before being assigned to a job.

Carissa shared the full plan with her LLNL team and asked for their ideas for a plan to rebuild the space. She did not tell them about the deal with the President and that she had the presidential authority to formulate and implement a US plan to restore the space domain. She asked the team to imagine a new space architecture, using the latest LLNL technologies in cube sats, advanced sensors, and space situational awareness to create a new, more robust, un-hackable satellite network to advance US commercial, military, and intelligence objectives, while at the same time ushering in a new era of international cooperation in the peaceful uses of space. No big deal. She was happy about the prospects for integrating her lab colleague's cutting-edge optics, which had proven so effective on the International Space Station, into the new network. "There's so much more we can do with the ISS," she thought to herself. "Maybe the ISS is the starting point for international cooperation."

At some point, Carissa knew she would have to level with Lucky. They were both implementing secret plans but on separate tracks. She needed to know his plans for making and launching the Silver Surfer rockets. How was Lucky planning to get the bots loaded into the Falcon 9 rockets? "I'll bet he and Yater are up to something."

Still feeling unsure about her new authorities, she called her Space Force friends at the ground-based tracking stations to warn them about what might appear to be a series of unplanned, unreported, and unauthorized launches. Jeff Clark at Half Moon Bay, Lance Hamilton in Maui, and Jake Burton in Colorado accepted her story without question. They were used to Carissa calling the shots when it came to rocket launches. "Whatever you need us to do, Carissa." "I need you to coordinate with the Aussies and NATO to advise them about an upcoming series of classified launches." "You got it, bro." Bro? Jesus.

Next, she called Gerry Lopez at Los Alamos to talk about using Oppie to characterize the radiation fields. He was also eager to follow her lead. "You got it, girl. Your Duke and my Oppie. Together, we're unbeatable." What a weird thing to say. I hope he's not weird, Carissa thought to herself. I sort of like him. No time for that anyway. She needed to close the circle with Eileen and Andrei to see if she could get the Chinese and the Russians on board. They could really help with the space cleanup, especially if they had decided against invading their neighbors. Was this even legal, she wondered? "Can I trust Keala to have my back?"

CHAPTER TWENTY

The Red Sparrow

"Eileen, can you come to my office?" "Uhhh... ok," Eileen replied, her voice shaking. Her palms started to sweat, and her heart was pounding like a jackhammer. "Oh my god, they know. I'm going to jail forever." Carissa greeted Eileen in the hall outside the operations center and, gently put her hand on her back and guided her down the hall to her office. "Please sit down, Eileen."

"Eileen, I want to get your ideas about a few things. Do you have a few minutes?"

"Uhh, yes, ok."

"Eileen, you are doing a fine job here. I value your contributions to the team. We all do. How do you think you are doing?"

"Uhh, pretty good, I guess."

"It's been pretty intense around here lately. How are you holding up? Are you taking care of yourself? Finding time to relax?"

"Dr. Moore, I need to tell you something."

"Sure, what's on your mind?"

"Dr. Moore, this isn't easy. Oh my god, I'm so embarrassed. I had no choice, I promise."

"What do you mean? Just spit it out, Eileen. What's up?"

"OK, I got in trouble at school in Hong Kong and some guys told me I had to go to school at Berkeley and get an internship at the Lab. All I have to do is text them about the lab. I don't tell them anything important. If I don't, they will arrest me and put me in jail. And my parents, and my brother. I'm so sorry, Dr. Moore. I didn't want to do it. I love you guys and the lab and the work we're doing. I'm so sorry." She was shaking.

"Okay, Eileen, calm down. Breathe. It's all going to be okay. A lot is going on, and you can really help us now. Here's what I need you to do. You text your handlers in China, right?"

"Yes. I'm so sorry. They forced me."

"It's fine. Listen to me. I want you to text them something that can help us and help the world. Can you do that?"

"I guess. I'm not sure. What do you want me to do?"

"Eileen, did you tell your MSS contacts in China about Quicksilver?"

"Yes, I did. I'm so sorry. And Duke and Oppie, too."

"It's fine. Now, I need you to tell them that the US is planning a bigger version of Quicksilver, and we want their help. Tell them that we want them to send a whole bunch of their Blossom Flower murder hornets into LEO to grab the debris that's endangering everything. They can also use the Shijian 21 to tow some of the big pieces away from the orbits. Tell them we are having private discussions about approaching their government."

"I guess I can do that. What about the aliens? Rell told me about it. I told them all about that, too. I'm so sorry."

"Excuse me?"

"Rell told me all about the secret program that collects alien spacecraft and their crews. I know it's super-secret. I told them about it. I'm so sorry."

Carissa could hardly keep a straight face.

"Yes, well, I guess the cat's out of the bag. Let's save that one for later. For now, we need to focus on cleaning up LEO. Can you text your buddies and tell them about our interest in a global effort to clean up space? You should mention that we are considering asking the Russians to join the effort. Can you do that?"

"Yes, Dr. Moore. I'm so sorry. I love you and the team, and I would never do anything to hurt you."

"It's fine, Eileen. Let's look to the future. Please let me know as soon as you contact them, especially if you get a response. Okay?"

"Yes, Dr. Moore. I can do that," she blubbered through the tears that were now flooding her pretty face. Carissa took her hands in hers and gave them a little squeeze. "It's going to be okay, Eileen. I promise." Then she led her back to her intern cubby and said, "Eileen, we have a chance to do something good and important. You are part of the team with an important role to play." Walking back to her office, Carissa thought to herself, "I'm a pretty good spymaster." Now to deal with Andrei and the Russians, and talk to Rell about aliens.

CHAPTER TWENTY-ONE

My Dinner with Andrei

Carissa called Andrei's burner phone number. "Carissa, I was hoping you would call. I have many ideas about how we can work together, but you have to get me out of here. They will think I'm a traitor. Can you get me out of here? It's all based on your research. We did the calculations. You were right, Carissa. You were right about the rivers in the sky."

"Okay, okay. Take a breath, Andrei. Let's figure it out. Do you have any academic conferences coming up? Anything in Europe? Or Asia?"

"Europe is hard, Carissa, after Ukraine. We are blocked from travel. How about India? There is the International Conference on Condensed Matter and Device Physics in Gujarat. It's coming up quickly. I would have to get permission. But our work would fit in the conference guidelines. It would not be suspicious. The Indians are still friends. They will issue a visa."

"Okay, Andrei. Register for the conference. I will meet you there."

"Carissa, my love. I cannot wait to see you."

"Whoa, down, buddy. This is about saving the world, not about romance."

"I understand, but I cannot control my feelings for you."

"Well, let's just take it one step at a time. Can you send me the research?"

"Yes, I can do that, but it would not be wise to send it to you directly. Do you have a secure communication channel?"

"I will send you a secure link, ostensibly for sharing academic research papers. Do you understand? It will appear to be from the Indian conference organizers."

"Yes, I understand, Carissa."

"Thank you, Andrei. And I need you to do one more thing for me. Who is your government contact at the institute? Do you have security officers who monitor your activities?"

"Yes, of course. The FSB, SVR, and GRU all meddle in our business. They are morons, Carissa, with nothing better to do than follow around a bunch of physicists and interfere in our work. They ask us the same questions over and over. They do not understand science. They think they own us. They think they own our work. They think they own science."

"That's good, Andrei. I need you to tell the security officers at your Institute that US experts do not understand the physics of space adequately and would need Russia's advanced understanding of space operations to restore LEO for peaceful and military applications. Just tell them that, as a matter of science, you do not believe the Americans will be able to address the problem of space debris without Russian assistance. As a matter of science."

"Will that not create suspicions?"

"You can say that, in your opinion, the situation favors Russia. You can say that Russia is in a position to take the lead in restoring its prominence in space ahead of the Americans."

"I see. Yes, I can do that, but they are morons, Carissa. Complete idiots."

"That's ok, Andrei. We need to send a message about what's coming next. We need to lay the groundwork for cooperation. We are doing this for both of our countries. We're doing it for the world."

"All right, my love. We will do it together. We will save the world together."

"We'll talk soon."

"Damn, I'm good at this," Carissa thought to herself. "I'm a pretty hot honey pot if I do say so myself. Poor Andrei. He's a hopeless romantic. I hope I can pull this off. I'm going to need help. I need to tell Lucky what's going on. And I need to tell the President."

What Carissa had in mind was to propose cooperating with Russia and China to clean up space. In addition to their vast experience and world-class operational capacity to assist the clean-up effort, Andrei's experimental data could turn her theories about the rivers of charged particles flowing through space into actual methods to move and possibly eliminate the debris fields. Not only could the Russians use their ASAT technologies to remove chunks of debris from orbit, like Quicksilver and Blossom Flower, but Carissa thought the President might like the idea of proposing world-saving scientific cooperation as part of her new space treaty initiative.

Maybe she could get China, Russia and the US to work together on a new era of cooperative threat reduction for space. She recalled how her colleagues at Livermore had cooperated with Russian scientists after the Cold War to secure former Soviet nuclear, chemical and biological weapons to keep them out of the hands of proliferators and terrorists. Other space-faring nations, like India and Japan, might want to join the effort. "I think we can do this," she told herself.

CHAPTER TWENTY-TWO

Games Without Frontiers

Eileen contacted her Ministry of State Security handlers and conveyed Carissa's message. They reported the message from one of their most valuable assets up through the PLA and CCP chain of command, where it landed on Xi's desk. The US would like to cooperate with Beijing and Moscow to clean up the mess in space. "Can it be true that the Americans want us to deploy our Blossom Flower technology to help clean up space?" Xi mused. The message appeared to come from Livermore National Lab, where Eileen, the spy, was embedded.

"Are the scientists acting on behalf of their government? Do they really want us to launch more ASATs to help remove debris from LEO? What do we get in exchange? How would that advance our objectives?"

Xi consulted with his inner circle of advisors. "Do we join with the Americans and Russians or seize the moment to achieve strategic advantage?"

The chairman of the Central Committee offered his perspective. "We would definitely benefit from a revitalized space domain environment. We are now positioned to benefit from space in ways that we were not prepared to exploit when the Americans and Russians made their space race the vanguard of their Cold War competition. In the new space race, we are in a position to win. This is also the case with nuclear competition. They are losing energy as we grow stronger."

Chen Wenwing, the Minister of State Security, whose officers were managing Eileen, offered another view. "Sir, what about the matter of the alien technologies? Perhaps we could offer to assist the international coalition in exchange for information about the aliens and their technologies. Extraterrestrial DNA could be very useful. We could offer to assist in the evaluation of the aliens, in the spirit of cooperation, of course."

"Interesting. Direct our Ambassador at the CD to make a quiet inquiry to the American representative, asking for details about their plans. Suggest the possibility that we recognize mutual interests in S&T cooperation in space policy."

In Moscow, Andrei approached the dingy office where Igor Penkovsky, the representative of the Foreign Intelligence Service (formerly the KGB, now known as the SVR), sat, leaning back in his metal chair, his feet up on the desk, smoking cigarettes, drinking vodka, and sleeping. Monitoring scientists at the Moscow Institute of Physics and Technology was not a prime assignment for an SVR officer, even if the Moscow Institute was an elite institution. Andrei had been avoiding the intelligence services for years. He considered them to be useless annoyances beneath him. Approaching the office, he rehearsed his pitch. Russia possesses a competitive advantage in space. The Americans do not understand certain scientific principles and have admitted as much in scientific exchanges. Russia has an opportunity to offer its advanced space capabilities in exchange for concessions. Our knowledge gives us leverage.

Penkovsky, a pock-faced, balding, disheveled, and overweight bureaucrat, impassively scribbled Andrei's report with a chewed pencil and weathered legal pad. "Anything else, Wasileski? Where did you get the idea that the Americans want our help?"

"We track the academic literature. They are speculating on things that we know very well but have not shared with them. They do not understand the electromagnetic forces affecting the debris fields in space. We are required to report to you any scientific breakthroughs that could have strategic consequences. This is such an opportunity. The

Americans cannot do these things. We could demand, for example, the lifting of sanctions in exchange."

Andrei was proud of this last flourish. He couldn't wait to tell Carissa. Penkovsky typed the report from his notes into his filthy, yellowed Soviet-era computer and sent it to the SVR's technical intelligence branch. Ironically, SVR technical managers forwarded the report to their experts – at the very same Moscow Institute of Physics and Technology – for analysis and evaluation. When his department chairman sent the report back to Andrei for evaluation, he shook his head and muttered, "Morons." He then dutifully assessed his intelligence report, calling it "indisputably accurate, timely, and actionable." The department chair sent Andrei's report back to SVR's technical branch, where it was classified as top secret and flagged for inclusion in the Kremlin's daily intelligence briefing report, roughly equivalent to the US President's Daily Brief.

In his daily briefing, Putin's intelligence chief mentioned the report that indicated that the scientists had identified a possible Russian advantage in the unfolding space disaster. "We may have capabilities that the Americans can only dream of, sir. We should consider how to use them to create a more favorable correlation of forces." "Yes," Putin mused. "We could offer our help in exchange for something of value, such as relief from the sanctions that they heaped on us for defending ourselves against Ukrainian and NATO aggression. Where did this information come from?"

"From one of our scientists who studies space phenomena, sir."

"Have our ambassador to the Conference on Disarmament inquire discreetly with the American representative regarding their needs. We might consider a deal."

"Yes, sir. I will convey your directive to the Foreign Ministry."

CHAPTER TWENTY-THREE

Revenge of the Nerds

Carissa called Lucky to level with him. "Lucky, we gotta talk," Carissa began what she feared would be a long and contentious conversation. Lucky was headstrong and might not take kindly to being told that there was a separate plan that he was not aware of – or controlling.

"What's up, buttercup?"

"Lucky, there's a bunch of things we have to discuss. Where are you right now?"

"I'm at Vandenberg. Do you need me to drive up to the lab? I have Dora with me."

"Yes, how fast can you get here?"

"A few hours if I don't stop and surf in Santa Cruz. Steamer Lane is pumping. I have my boards. I was thinking of calling Jeff Clark at Mavericks. I need to talk to him anyway. What's up?"

"Can you come here first and surf later? Why don't you meet me at my house? I'll cook dinner."

Lucky arrived in his spacy silver Tesla pick-up truck, a prototype gifted to him by his frenemy Elon Musk, accompanied by his dog Dora.

Lucky pulled into Carissa's driveway in the Oakland hills. Her shingled cottage was perched on the hillside, surrounded by eucalyptus and redwood trees, with peek-through views of the San Francisco Bay. The trees were a fire hazard, she knew, but she couldn't bring herself to cut them down. She loved how they looked and smelled and how they cradled her in nature. Carissa cooked teriyaki turkey burgers on the grill, topped with avocados and bacon, and poured two full glasses of

Wente vineyard chardonnay. "Lucky, there's a lot to discuss. I know you have your super-sized Quicksilver plan going. I'm on board with it. What I wanted to tell you is that the President asked me to help her deal with the space mess. That includes your clean-up plan. She wants to help."

"Help how? Space Force and SPACECOM told me to go fuck myself. Yater retired and went to work for SpaceX. I'm doing it all off the books, paying for the bots myself. What's the President going to do about that?"

"Well, can you make enough of the Quicksilver satellites?"

"I'm making a few dozen at my Palmdale facility, and SpaceTech is making another dozen or so. It's not enough, but it's a start. I wouldn't mind getting paid, and I sure would like to avoid getting prosecuted for stealing government technology."

"And how are you planning to get them into LEO? Do you have a deal to launch them?"

"Sorta, kinda, not really. I'll level with you, Carissa. Yater is at SpaceX to get access to a Falcon 9 that's on the launch pad at Vandenberg. It's slated to launch an NRO payload. We're basically planning on hijacking it."

"Jesus Lucky. And how are you planning to get the satellites loaded on the Falcon 9? Sneak them onto the base, then what?"

"Well, I've talked to some of my SEAL buddies, and Yater, and some of the Space Force guys. We think we could bring them in from the sea on a barge. We would load the barge in Point Hueneme or Ventura and drag it up the coast to Vandenberg. I could do it with my boat. It's big enough. The launch pad is really close to the beach. Some of the guys have surfed there. We can carry the bots to the launch pad and load them ourselves. They're not that heavy. I think it's doable."

Carissa stared in disbelief at Lucky, who was sitting across from her on the other side of the wood slab table, grinning in his trademark orange Hawaiian shirt, Volcom shorts and Rainbow sandals. Dora, the dog, snorted for scraps under the table. After a long pause, she spoke.

"You're fucking insane, Lucky. Certifiably, fucking insane. What's your plan? Pack a barge full of homemade satellites and beach it at a Space Force base, where you steal a rocket and go for a joyride. That's it?"

"Look, I know there are a few loose ends, but somebody has to do something, Carissa. I'm not going to sit on my ass while everything we worked for and dreamed about is trashed like a fucking demolition derby. If the government isn't going to fix it, I can at least try."

"How many Claw bots can you fit in a Falcon9?"

"Eight or ten. They're reusable, so we could land it somewhere and send up another load. That gets us to about twenty. I figured that when the government sees that it works, they will stop trying to block us and get on board. We could use more bots and more launches. Think of it as a proof of concept."

"Jesus Lucky."

"You already said that. Those two things don't really go together, do they? Jesus and Lucky."

"Here's what I need you to do. Make as many Quicksilver bots as you can, but don't steal a rocket, okay? I'll talk to the President and see if we can get the launches you need. We don't need a bunch of SEALs and surfers landing a pirate barge on the beach at Vandenberg in the middle of the night and hijacking a Falcon9 from Space Force. For God's sake, Lucky. That's nuts."

"How long? We can't wait. That's why I came up with this plan. The government takes forever, and we need to clean up the mess now. We have to try. It's sort of a moral responsibility. You know what I mean?"

"Yeah, it didn't take long before we trashed space. At least it took a few hundred years for us to pollute the environment here on Earth. It only took a few decades to destroy space. Humans are good at wrecking things."

"Like the Joni Mitchell song: 'They paved paradise and put up a parking lot.' It's true. You don't know what you've lost till it's gone. Humans suck."

"Let me talk to Keala, I mean the President, and see if we can get some top cover for our plan."

"Keala? Do you call the President Keala? Are you and the President a thing? I didn't think you were gay. So it's our plan now?"

"I'm not gay, and we're not together like that. But she gets me, and we are becoming pretty good friends. It's weird. But yes, Lucky, it's our plan now, so let's be honest with each other. I should tell you some other things that are happening. I'm trying to get the Chinese and Russians to help. Maybe the Indians as well."

"That would help if they would use their nasty ASAT shit to help clean up the mess they made. Good luck to you and the President. You're as crazy as me, Carissa. You're one badass nerd."

They clinked wine glasses, finished the bottle, and opened another as they sat on Carissa's deck and watched the sun set into the Pacific through the trees. They were good friends and co-conspirators.

CHAPTER TWENTY-FOUR

Friends in High Places

Carissa called the President on her private line to update her on the plans to clean up LEO. She was stunned when President Kennelly answered the phone. "Hello, Carissa. What have you got for me?" Carissa described Lucky's plan for a super-sized Quicksilver program but excluded details about his plan to steal a rocket from a military base. Instead, she asked the President to authorize several designated launches of sensitive cargo. She disclosed how Lucky was making more Quicksilver satellites and needed heavy lift launches to get them into orbit. He would need access to the rockets to secure the payloads. The President agreed to direct SPACECOM to order the Space Force to prepare a series of launches of special cargo from Vandenberg.

Carissa described her covert communications with China and Russia, using Eileen and Andrei to ask for their help in cleaning up LEO.

"I may need to go to a conference in India to meet my contact. Is that okay? He wants to defect and help us. Can I get some help with that?"

"Yes, I'll have CIA Director Peterson contact you to arrange it. What about your Chinese asset?"

"She's scared but happy to help. I just need her not to be arrested for espionage. I guess you should warn the FBI and our counterintelligence office at the lab."

"You're quite the spymaster, Carissa. Perhaps you missed your calling; you would have made a great case officer."

"Is that a compliment?" Carissa replied dryly. "And you have an awesome sense of humor," the President added.

President Kennelly gathered her thoughts. She would direct the State Department to be on the lookout for diplomatic openings to engage Moscow and Beijing on space cooperation, especially at the Conference on Disarmament in Geneva, where space policy was a hot topic and high on the agenda. Ambassador Marks, the former professional surfer and Navy SEAL, might have some ideas. Carissa described how Chinese and Russian ASAT capabilities and their ample launch services could greatly expedite the clean-up effort. She briefly mentioned that Russian scientific innovations might produce a helpful breakthrough in space technology.

"That's why I need to go to India," she added awkwardly.

"Because the Russians stole your research, and you're going to get it back?" Keala quipped admiringly.

"Yes, something like that," Carissa answered.

The President told Carissa that she would instruct the intelligence community (IC) to prioritize the collection of all-source reporting on Russian and Chinese discussions about space cooperation and competition. Were Putin and Xi sincere about cooperating or merely seeking tactical advantage? Intelligence reporting could reveal their true intentions. "We might also pick up something about your spies," she said hopefully. Was there anything else the IC should be looking for? Carissa suggested including India on the list of possible partners. Intelligence reporting might indicate whether they would be willing to join the multilateral effort.

The President added, "We have very reliable reporting on Xi and Modi's thinking about their stupid war that neither of them wanted. Both are looking for a way out. Maybe they will see global space cooperation and the new treaty as good ways to rehabilitate their reputations."

"I hope so, but I wouldn't get my hopes up. My dad always said that leopards don't change their spots, although I think he was referring to the Nationals replacing the Senators." Carissa replied."

"Thank you, Carissa. This is exactly what I need – keep going. I have your back."

"I sure hope so." Carissa thought to herself. "Otherwise, I'm screwed."

CHAPTER TWENTY-FIVE

The Tao of Physics

Carissa was excited to attend the physics conference in India. She had dreamed about going to India and maybe attending a yoga retreat and visiting the abundant spiritual landmarks. The International Conference on Condensed Matter and Device Physics was being held in Gujarat, home to a rich tradition of arts and culture, and Gir National Park, one of the only places in the world to see lions in their natural habitat. It was also the birthplace of Mahatma Gandhi. Her mom and dad used to talk about Gandhi's influence on Martin Luther King.

Andrei, however, was terrified. The arrangements for his defection gave him night terrors. What if he was caught? What if the SVR was following him and listening to his calls? At the President's direction, Carissa had met with CIA Director Lakey Peterson and her team from the Directorate of Operations, the folks who conduct covert activities. This would be a case of exfiltration, where the asset is removed from the field and given a new identity in the US. Andrei, the team explained, would have a new job as a physics professor at Cal State Fresno, a state school in the Central Valley. In addition, he would have a hefty travel budget and a generous consulting contract with Lawrence Livermore Lab, to make it easy for him to collaborate with Carissa and the scientists there. It was a sweet deal, but Andrei was nervous. "Will you also live in Fresno with me?" he asked Carissa when she called to lay out the plan. "No, Andrei, but Fresno is beautiful," she lied. She had driven through the Central Valley a few times and hated it. It was flat, hot, and very white, she recalled. Lots of Trump flags. She ate at a restaurant called Cracker Barrel. What else was there to say? "It's an easy drive to the Bay Area, Andrei. You'll love it."

Exfiltration would be relatively easy. The conference was in Gandhinagar, on the outskirts of the major city of Ahmedabad. Before the lunch break on the last day of the conference, Andrei would leave the plenary session and go to the restroom, where CIA officers would whisk him out the back entrance of the conference hotel, into a waiting car, and escort him to the Mumbai airport, where he would present his new US passport to board a commercial flight direct to San Francisco. There, he would debrief a team of technical experts from the IC and the national labs on his research into Carissa's theories. Carissa had explained it to Andrei several times and reassured him that everything would work according to plan, but he was as nervous as a chipmunk.

6"I'll be there with you, Andrei. Don't worry." No yoga or lions on this trip, Carissa lamented.

But a new development had arisen from the intelligence reporting, according to the CIA team. Several prominent Indian and Chinese scientists who worked on classified programs will be attending the conference.

Would Carissa be willing to approach them? Patty, her CIA handler, asked, "You know how to talk to scientists. Maybe you could engage them in a conversation that elicits insights into their work. You might talk to them about the difficulty of funding big science projects or the restrictions on their travel and publications."

"I can do that. No problem. I like talking to scientists about their work."

"This chick is a rock star!" Patty told her CIA colleagues.

The conference unfolded according to plan. Andrei and several other Russian physicists arrived without incident on the Aeroflot flight from Moscow. His colleagues had longstanding relationships with Indian scientists. They had been to India before and had hosted their Indian counterparts at their institutes in Russia. They liked India. They were comfortable. Andrei was miserable. Stepping off the plane in Mumbai, the smothering heat hit him like a punch in the gut, and the smell of diesel and rotting garbage roiled his already clenched stomach, leaving him hunched over and panting. The ride to the conference hotel through the legendary slums of Mumbai left him shaken, and the freezing air conditioning inside the van iced the sweat on his temples and made him shiver. He thought he might pass out. The hotel room was adequate, but the air conditioning was arctic, and he hated curry.

"Everything smells like fucking curry. I hate curry. I hate this place."

He took a shower and unthinkingly gulped tepid water from the shower head as it dribbled onto his upturned face. By the time he dressed and took the elevator down to the lobby to meet Carissa for dinner, his stomach was churning, preparing to explode. He didn't know where the contents of his stomach would exit first, his mouth or his butt, but it was coming out. Nobody told him not to drink the water.

Carissa's flight to Mumbai was blissfully uneventful. The CIA had arranged for her to fly business class, direct from SFO, and she had a suite with a view of the city. Not bad. She arrived a few hours before Andrei and had time to shower and change before meeting him in the lobby. When she saw Andrei emerge from the elevator, she almost laughed. He looked terrible. His skin was green, he was hunched over and sweaty. What happened to the brilliant and arrogant young physicist who commanded the forces of nature with his mind? She had never seen this side of him, and she didn't like it. He smelled like the parakeet cage in her aunt's living room in Baltimore. Pathetic. Not sexy.

But she hugged him, thanked him for coming, and told him how happy she was to see him. The bedraggled Andrei forced a smile and apologized for his appearance.

"I don't feel good, Carissa."

"You look fine, Andrei. Welcome to India."

Neither of them noticed the surveillance teams that were observing their awkward reunion. But Carissa's CIA team noticed the Russian SVR, Indian RAW and Chinese MSS security officers stationed throughout the elaborate hotel lobby, surveilling them.

"This might not be as easy as we thought," Patty, the leader of the American team, acknowledged.

"There's more interest in Andrei than we expected."

"Do you want to sit on the veranda and get some air?" Carissa gently asked Andrei.

"Yes, that would be good. Thank you."

"We don't have to eat if you're not hungry. It's okay."

She led him by his sweaty hand out to the stone patio that was surrounded by lush and fragrant trees, overlooking the lighted swimming pool. Immediately, as if he had materialized from the stone patio, a tall, thin Tamil waiter in a white colonial officer's uniform with gold shoulder epaulets and a feathered cap appeared. "Good evening, sir and madam. May I bring you anything?" Carissa ordered a gin and tonic with extra lime and no ice. Andrei ordered vodka on the rocks.

"No ice," Carissa corrected, having been warned multiple times by her mentor, George, not to drink the water or eat raw vegetables.

Recalling his bout with Delhi belly years earlier, he told her, "I wouldn't eat a potato chip in India, even if it was deep fried. Keep your mouth and eyes shut in the shower, never eat salad, check the seals on bottled water, and watch out for ice in drinks, even if they tell you it's safe. They refill the water bottles with a hose out back."

The waiter straightened, cocked his chin as if to salute, and pivoted on his heel like a real soldier.

"Yes, sir. Thank you, ma'am."

"How are you holding up, Andrei?"

"Not so good. I'm sorry, Carissa."

"Andrei, it's fine. We're going to get through this, no problem. The conference agenda looks really good. What panels do you want to attend? It looks like there are a few excellent presentations. Did you see the one on laser photonics? I'm looking forward to the poster sessions. The Indians are doing lots of interesting research on charged particles in ultra-low temperature environments."

"I may just be in my room, shitting and barfing. Do we have to stay here? Can we escape sooner?"

"Maybe. I can check. Did you bring your data, or do you have access to it? I'm eager to hear what you found out about my theories. You stole my ideas, you bastard."

"Yes, I have it on a thumb drive. I took it from the lab at the institute. But I'm afraid they're watching me, Carissa. I told the SVR, as you said. I told them Russia has an advantage in space. They sent the report back to me to evaluate my work. They are fucking idiots but also ruthless. I don't think we are safe here."

The fake soldier brought their drinks with a bowl of chili cashews and placed them on the glass table between their white rattan chairs. Carissa thanked him and signed the tab with her room number.

"I wonder if the CIA is covering my bar tab?" she thought to herself.

"I like gin and tonic."

"Don't worry, Andrei. I'm sorry you don't feel well. We don't have to go to dinner. Why don't you go back to your room and go to bed? We'll reconvene when the presentations begin tomorrow. Okay? Get some sleep."

"I guess. Do you want to come to bed with me? I missed you."

"You get some sleep, and I'll meet you here in the morning, in the lobby."

They finished their drinks and returned to their rooms. As Carissa perused the room service menu, she heard a soft knock on her door. Through the peephole, she saw Patty, the head of the CIA team. She opened the door and let her in.

"FYI, Carissa, the hotel is crawling with surveillance. We ID'd SVR, MSS, RAW, and god knows who else is watching you and Andrei in the lobby. That was pathetic, by the way."

"I know, he's not the same guy I knew. He's sort of disgusting, but he's got the information."

"Good. Just be aware that you're under a microscope. You don't need to do anything, but just be aware. Here are the scientists we'd like you to engage if possible," pointing to a few Chinese and Indian names on the conference registration list.

"Are you still up for it?"

"Sure," she replied breezily. "I don't mind talking to them. They're nerds like me."

The physics conference proceeded like every other international scientific meeting, with crowds of socially awkward and oddly dressed scientific researchers enthusiastically exchanging ideas about arcane subjects. It didn't matter if they were in India, Argentina, or Timbuktu – they were all fluent in the international language of physics and chemistry and happy to be with their community, their tribe of like-minded individuals. This was their Comic Con, Burning Man, and Jazz Fest, a chance to geek out with people who understood them better than non-scientists, including their friends and family. These were their people.

Carissa attended a panel on spintronic and diluted magnetic semiconductors and one on electronic structures and phonons, which she genuinely enjoyed. Andrei felt good enough to attend several panels, even asking a few know-it-all questions to the panelists. Carissa easily struck up conversations with the Indian and Chinese scientists on her CIA to-do list, engaging them during the tea breaks about their research and funding. She invited them to be in touch with her about possible collaboration and exchanged business cards, which she gave to Patty. "That girl is a natural," Patty told her team. "We should recruit her."

When the time came for Andrei to make his vanishing bathroom act, the exfiltration team had prepared a few twists to distract the foreign agents. When he left the meeting room at the tea break, Carissa would take a walk in the opposite direction, out to the white stone veranda and do some yoga stretching by the pool. Patty knew the Russian, Chinese and Indian intelligence officers, all men, could not resist the temptation of watching an attractive young and exotic American woman doing sexy yoga poses by the pool. Carissa agreed to play the role, even wearing her stretchy Prana yoga slacks that highlighted the contours of her spectacular round ass and showed a hint of her thong underwear lines. "Why not? I was hoping to do some yoga in India."

"I love this chick!" Patty told her team. "She's got balls!" Then, for good measure, Patty paid a group of kids to light off a bunch of high-power fireworks right outside the hotel lobby. With the crush of scientists seeking their tea and snacks, Carissa contorting her body by the pool, and the street urchins adding pyrotechnics to the commotion, Andrei took his bathroom break, had a quick bout of diarrhea, strolled to the rear entrance of the hotel, out to the loading dock, where Patty's exfiltration team made him disappear, like a David Copperfield magic show in Vegas. Poof. Gone.

CHAPTER TWENTY-SIX

The Smoore Flow

Andrei was happy to land in the Bay Area. The CIA put him up in a suite in the Claremont, a luxurious spa hotel near UC Berkeley, where he made good use of the massage, sauna, room services and pay-per-view porn movies. His debriefing sessions were mind-blowing for the US experts from the IC and national labs who gathered at Lawrence Livermore National Lab to hear his stories. Andrei proudly described the experiments the Russians had conducted using Carissa's theoretical calculations.

The Russians had sent specialized sensors into space to locate, characterize and map Carissa's electromagnetic rivers. Not only did they exist, but the Russian scientists had used X-ray laser pulses to energize the particle rivers with the intent to weaponize them against US space operations. The electromagnetic rivers, it turned out, could be charged and directed at objects in space, like satellites. Andrei's revelations raised eyebrows among some of the IC debriefers, who immediately connected the experimental results with mysterious pulses they had detected first at the Novaya Zemla nuclear test site and later flowing outward from LEO to GEO but could not explain. US spy satellites had registered what looked like the Northern lights on steroids glowing beyond the atmosphere, but they could only add the sightings to the list of unexplained phenomena. Carissa listened with her arms crossed, trying not to appear smug. She knew she was right.

Carissa also knew that somebody would take credit for the discovery, so she took the opportunity to name the phenomenon after her dad, Samuel Moore. Off the top of her head, she referred to the phenomena as the Smoore Flow. The other technical debriefers in the room accepted it without comment. Only Andrei reacted with a quizzical look; he had hoped to name it after himself. Recognizing Andrei's desire for recognition, Carissa asked him if he would like to give a lecture at the Lab on his research findings. He accepted happily.

The implications of the Smoore Flow were profound on many levels. Scientifically, it confirmed the permeability of the supposed layers of the outer atmosphere, as Carissa had postulated. Rivers of charged particles were indeed flowing outward from Earth, through LEO and MEO, out to GEO. There was so much to learn about them. Her head was spinning thinking about the Russian research and how the Flow could be studied -- and used. Bureaucratically, the Flow muddled the areas of responsibility claimed by numerous US military and intelligence agencies, as had been predicted by the LLNL-NRO wargame, which now seemed like a distant memory. Who's in charge of the Flow?

Strategically, the Russian findings further blurred the lines between offense and defense due to the potential for the Flow to be weaponized. If we can control it, it can be used for good or for evil. She wondered if the Flow might have implications for planetary defense against rogue asteroids if the rivers could be transformed to act as directed energy beams. Perhaps they could be lit up with high-power lasers. For the purpose of cleaning up orbital debris, however, Carissa was optimistic that the Smoore Flow could be used to move and possibly disintegrate space junk.

Perhaps with the right laser energies, even small debris particles could be zapped by the Flow. Perhaps directing the Flow could be the catalyst for cooperation that the President was looking for. The Russians were doing it already, and the Chinese and Indians probably knew about it. Our allies will be interested, for sure. Perhaps the whole world can agree on a plan to clean up space, using the Blossom Flower murder hornets, Quicksilver, and the Flow. Maybe the reconstruction effort could be guided by the State Department's new space treaty. Perhaps. Carissa couldn't wait to share the news with Keala.

The experts assigned to debrief Andrei agreed on the revolutionary potential of the Smoore Flow. It could be a game-changer. Collectively, they agreed to commission a study by the National Academy of Sciences, which would recommend a path forward for the research community. Every US government agency recognized the implications of the Flow for their mission. Job one was the clean-up. Then would come the task of reimagining and repopulating the space domain, first for national security, then for international prosperity.

CHAPTER TWENTY-SEVEN

Mission Creep

The disaster in space and the new knowledge about the space domain presented an opportunity to design, develop, build and launch a new generation of resilient, hack-proof, maneuverable, Flow compatible, persistent, small, integrated, replaceable, serviceable, multi-sensor satellites. The top priority for the Pentagon, however, was to replace the damaged GPS with a new positioning and timing system to ensure navigation and targeting for all of the armed services. Its Joint All Domain Command and Control (JADCC) system was the key to modern warfare, and it depended on massive data flows from millions of sensors located throughout the space, air, land, and sea domains.

The Army, Navy, Air Force, Marines, and Coast Guard all wanted their own dedicated ISR and communications networks to support their operations. Special Operations Command in Tampa had developed operational concepts for small teams of Green Berets and SEALs operating in isolated areas to have their dedicated satellite constellations like the private sector was providing for companies.

This was their opportunity to catch up. Not since the founding of the Defense Department and the CIA in 1947, and perhaps after 9-11, had there been such open-mindedness about the roles and missions of all the US government security agencies.

The readiness and reliability of the conventional forces were also closely linked to STRATCOM's integrated nuclear deterrence posture and the guarantee that a nuclear attack on the US or its treaty allies would result in unacceptable damage to anyone foolish enough to contemplate taking such risks. The new space architecture improved ISR, and JADCC would make it possible for commanders and the President to calibrate the American response to war and escalation with greater precision.

SPACECOM needed more of everything. Within days of the crisis, the Commander ordered a quadrupling of its 75th Intelligence, Surveillance and Reconnaissance Squadron. The new national security architecture would include greatly expanded offensive and defensive capabilities, with small, maneuverable cube sats able to zoom around to attack and defend vital assets. The Smoore Flow might help. Quicksilver and the X-37B were just the beginning. The Air Force drafted a new plan to defend the upper atmosphere, including Very Low Earth Orbit (VLEO), with a new generation of high-flying drones, hypersonic missiles, and high-altitude aircraft. SPACECOM requested one hundred new X-37Cs. No longer content to sit back and defend US space assets, SPACECOM was going on offense.

The National Geospatial Agency (NGA) doubled down on its leading role, working with private vendors and academic partners to revolutionize the collection and analysis of geospatial intelligence (GEOINT) information using AI to cull massive amounts of data from multi-spectral platforms capable of covering every inch of the Earth at any moment. The National Security Agency (NSA) had already designed a next-generation signals intelligence (SIGINT) system capable of collecting and sorting any type of communications from across the electromagnetic spectrum. Here, too, AI and machine learning would help IC analysts find valuable nuggets of information in the global cacophony of human chatter.

CYBERCOM provided insights into how to make the new satellite networks and their data streams hack-proof with quantum encryption, laser communications, digital twins and other new concepts for data integrity. NRO's new and improved Silent Barker space surveillance would employ all of these concepts to ensure there would be plenty of warning about covert space activities, like secret moon bases and sneak attacks.

The Department of Energy and the National Nuclear Security Agency (NNSA) developed a new generation of sensors to detect nuclear testing and covert proliferation to replace the old "bhang meters" that had been damaged by the space war. To support these missions, the national labs designed a vast array of new concept multi-spectral sensors, advanced optics, lasers, synthetic aperture radars, novel materials, and other emerging technologies, including new systems to help agencies such as the Defense Advanced Research Projects Agency (DARPA) explore and exploit the Smoore Flow phenomena for national security applications. The spin-offs from these innovations would have widespread but unpredictable applications.

The CIA, which had managed the exfiltration of Andrei and his research findings, established new programs to track foreign space programs, including their supply chains and S&T investments. The reconstruction of the space domain would present many opportunities. One early benefit came from the FBI tracking of Eileen's text messages to her MSS handlers, which revealed an extensive network of Chinese agents at American labs, companies, and universities.

Other agencies would benefit as well. NASA would integrate the new systems into its programs, including plans for the ISS, the Hubble and Webb space telescopes, and its manned space missions. These civilian programs, Carissa recognized, would be central to any international cooperation. The Department of Commerce would facilitate relations with private companies wanting to benefit from the new space economy. There would also be new export controls and regulations for the businesses associated with the reconstruction of space, especially after Kramer's Congressional testimony. The Treasury Department would oversee the massive investments, taxation, and fiscal policies required by the surge of global capital that was spending trillions on the emerging space infrastructure. With the international economy awakening from its slumber, a renaissance of repressed business energy was unleashed. The private sector didn't need encouragement from the government to rebuild the economy, but it did need guardrails.

Carissa's mentor, George Downing, saw the broader implications. It would take a coordinated, whole-of-government policy to fix the space domain and rebuild the global economy. This was unprecedented in human history, a chance to restructure the global economy for the benefit of all mankind. "This is a revolution," he told Carissa. "If we do this right, we can control climate change. We can correct structural shortages of energy and food. We can end poverty. I'm not kidding, Carissa. Tell your friend, the President that we need to draft a bold national strategy showing how all the pieces fit together. The people will love it. The whole world will love it."

Carissa prepared to report it all to the President. The new space architecture was the key to saving the planet. And the Smoore Flow could be the catalyst for cooperation in space.

CHAPTER TWENTY-EIGHT

Space Diplomacy

Carissa called the President to update her on Quicksilver, Silver Surfer, and the Smoore Flow. Quicksilver was progressing as planned. Lucky was cranking out the new clean-up bots in Palmdale and at SpaceTech. He had added a few upgrades suggested by Carissa, like advanced optics and sensors from Livermore lab. Yater had started his Skill Bridge transition at SpaceX and was relieved when he heard that the President had authorized the use of the Falcon 9 rockets to deliver the Quicksilver and Silver Surfer satellites to clear out LEO, so he wouldn't have to be part of Lucky's crazy conspiracy. Lucky was also relieved to learn that he could simply deliver the finished payloads to Vandenberg on trucks, and the Space Force payload experts would load them without the need for his madcap surfer-SEAL beach landing/infiltration operation. Ambassador Marks, the former professional surfer and SEAL, was amused by the plan when Carissa told her about it. "You nerds really are crazy," she told Carissa.

Lucky delivered the new and improved satellites to Vandenberg, where the Guardians loaded them on the first Falcon 9 without incident. The launch was flawless. Space Force tracking sites used LLNL coordinates to deliver the first dozen bots to precise locations in LEO, where they motored to their designated debris fields and started grabbing the largest pieces of junk and consolidating them. The Falcon 9 returned to base in-tact and readied for additional loads. It was a good start.

At the CD in Geneva, the Chinese ambassador caught Ambassador Marks during a coffee break and casually told her, "We have some things in common, Ambassador Marks. We were both athletes before starting our diplomatic careers."

"That's true. I understand that you are an accomplished martial artist. What style did you practice?"

"Ah, I'm a bit of a traditionalist. I studied at the Fukien Shaolin temple in the southern tradition, but I favor Yang-style tai chi for daily practice. Do you know of it?"

"Sorry, I learned my combat skills in the Navy. I was more of a surfer than a fighter, to be honest. Do you still practice?"

"Yes, but I've been out of shape since my movie actor days. I try to keep it up. You are welcome to join me if you would like. I lead a small class in the mornings, down by the lake."

"That is awfully kind of you, Ambassador Yen. I'm not in top shape either, I'm afraid. Too many pastries in Geneva. I haven't surfed in months."

"Please, call me Donnie. May I call you Caroline?"

"Yes, by all means, Donnie. Call me Caroline." She knew this was more than a social interaction. He was leading up to something.

"Caroline, my government supports global efforts to restore the space environment."

"That's good news, Donnie. Perhaps your government might be interested in pursuing cooperative measures, perhaps in the context of a new global space treaty?" She set the hook.

"We are interested, Caroline, in the modalities of how such cooperative measures might be realized. As you know, we possess certain capabilities, as do you, and the Russians, and others, that might be aligned to achieve our shared interests in the remediation of the space domain."

"I'm happy to hear that, Donnie. There are, indeed, many avenues through which to achieve our common objects in space. We could start with a joint draft space treaty. Beyond that, we might consider some form of technical cooperation. Would that be of interest?"

"My government is interested in a broad range of political, diplomatic, and scientific cooperation. There are many mysteries that we would be wise to face together rather than separately. The universe holds our common destiny."

"Indeed it does, Donnie. Indeed, it does. Would you like to propose some draft treaty language and perhaps suggest some burden-sharing in the clean-up efforts? Your SJ-21 mobile satellites could be particularly useful."

She wanted to say, "You know, the murder hornets that you unleashed on our Silent Barker space surveillance network." But she chose more diplomatic language.

"Yes, Caroline, a combined effort would be most efficient. We might also cooperate on our shared understanding of other extra-terrestrial phenomena, such as technologies or biologics that might originate from beyond our solar system or galaxy."

"Are you referring to planetary defense, because that is indeed a fruitful area for cooperation. I would be happy to convey that suggestion to my government." What the fuck is he talking about?

"Yes, planetary defense could be relevant in connection with the discovery of extra-terrestrial technologies."

"I'm not sure what you are talking about, Donnie."

"I'm referring to information about recovered alien spacecraft and their crew. We understand that your government is in possession of certain artifacts. Access to this evidence could greatly facilitate cooperation on other space matters."

Ambassador Marks had not been briefed on Rell Sunn's practical joke on Eileen, the Chinese spy at Livermore, so she didn't know that the Chinese leadership had been pranked into thinking that the US government was in possession of genuine aliens.

"Well, Donnie, I will report your interest in such artifacts. In the meantime, perhaps we can get started on a draft treaty. What do you think?"

"I, too, will report your receptivity to a wide range of scientific endeavors in the space domain. Thank you, Caroline. And please do join me for a little chi gong and tai chi session – every morning at 6:45 at the Parc de la Perle du Lac. I hope to see you there."

Caroline could hardly contain her laughter as she returned to the Assembly Hall. Had the Chinese ambassador lost his marbles? Space aliens? What the fuck? She couldn't wait to write the cable back to the State Department reporting on this conversation. The Secretary would get a kick out of it. They think we are sitting on a treasure trove of space aliens. Maybe they want to visit Area 51 or Roswell, New Mexico. What are they watching, the SyFy Channel? Congressional hearings? It's wacky, but it's a start.

As she was leaving the Palais de Nations to go home at the end of the day, the Russian ambassador caught Caroline near the elaborate, flag-lined entrance.

"Madam Marks. May I have a moment?" What now?

"How may I help you, Ambassador Gagarin?"

"Yes, please, a moment of your time. I have information that may be of value to you."

"I'm listening."

"My government regrets the situation that has negatively affected the space environment."

She wanted to say, "Yeah, because you assholes teamed up with the fucking Chinese to launch a sneak attack on us, and it failed. Now you're in deep shit and need our help to unfuck the mess you made." But instead, she used more diplomatic language.

"Thank you, Mr. Ambassador. I appreciate those sentiments." He continued.

"Our two countries have cooperated in the past to lead the world in space exploration. My government would like to engage in such cooperation once again as we remove the unfortunate pollution that impedes the peaceful uses of the space domain."

"That is very good news, Ambassador Gagarin. What type of cooperation do you have in mind? It's a big job."

"We understand that your government has come into possession of certain documentation of research conducted by our scientists into electromagnetic energy transport in the orbital regions."

Caroline wanted to say, "Yeah, you mean the information your spy stole from Livermore Lab that we got back? You mean the scientific information that you were trying to turn into an offensive weapon, like your secret biological weapons program?" But she used more diplomatic language to say:

"American and Russian scientists have often cooperated in space research and discovery, as you say. We, too, look forward to a resumption of our scientific collaboration, in space and in other areas of affecting our shared destiny. We might start by dedicating ourselves to abiding by a set of principles prohibiting the kind of aggression that produced the current circumstances." She couldn't resist a little jab.

"I quite agree, Madam Ambassador. A statement of principles would indeed help to guide the peaceful uses of space. In that regard, we would view the return of our scientist and the data he stole as a sign of good faith. Furthermore, the removal of the illegitimate sanctions imposed on us could open the door to mutually beneficial space operations, such as the clearing of debris. Such actions might be viewed as a starting point for cooperation to address the unfortunate orbital disturbances."

She wanted to say, "Let me get this straight. You want us to remove the sanctions imposed as a result of your unprovoked aggression against Ukraine and return the scientist who stole research from our labs in return for unspecified future opportunities to work with Russia on things we already do better than you? Go fuck yourself." But she used more diplomatic language to say, "I will convey your thoughts to my government, Oleg." She couldn't resist the implied insult of calling him by his first name.

It had been a long day. But rather than going home to her apartment and having a glass of wine, she went to the American embassy to write a long cable about her interactions with her Chinese and Russian counterparts. Clearly, they were interested in some form of cooperation, but it would be up to US policymakers to determine how to pull it all together. Drafting a treaty would be easy. Coordinating a multi-national effort to clean up space would be harder. But the hard work had begun.

Back in California, sitting on Carissa's deck in the Oakland hills, Lucky, Rell, Eileen, Andrei, Yater and Jeff Clark shared a laugh over how events had started to go their way. Who could have imagined? Quicksilver was working, and Silver Surfer was underway. The President of the United States was supporting their plans.

"It's a do-over like I wanted after Carissa's game," Lucky said to his friends.

"You jerk, it wasn't my game. It was our game." Carissa complained.

CHAPTER TWENTY-NINE

The Anarchic Society

The political theorist Hedley Bull described the restive combination of cooperation and competition in international affairs as an "anarchic society." The world is a dysfunctional family. The Chinese and the Russians wanted to cooperate but were also seeking opportunities to gain an advantage in space. Hearing about the successful exfiltration of Andrei and his confirmation of the Smoore Flow and Ambassador Marks' cable about Chinese and Russian entreaties in Geneva, President Kennelly decided it was time for another chat with her counterparts in Beijing and Moscow, hoping to lock down their cooperation.

Intelligence reporting had confirmed their interest in cleaning up LEO. They were also apparently open to the idea of a new space treaty, although they were both already violating the spirit and the letter of the proposed treaty with secret offensive programs, including the Blossom Flower moon base. No matter. They might be persuaded to give up their plans to invade their neighbors, at least for now, and help clean up the space mess. Eyes on the prize, President Kennelly told herself.

The President first called America's closest allies, Japan, Australia, and South Korea in Asia, and key NATO partners in Europe to consolidate plans for the reconstructed space architecture and the reinforced deterrence strategy for the space domain. The goal would be to establish respected global norms for space – the cooperation part of her strategy – while creating strong disincentives for competitors such as China and Russia to take the kind of risks that had led to the destruction of the space commons. Lingering hopes that global markets would have a civilizing effect on Moscow and Beijing had been dashed, which made the job of consolidating allies easier. The President would also have to call the Prime Minister of India, who was still trying to play both sides of each other but also served as a useful counterbalance to China. It was time for him to decide which side he was on.

The call to Xi was almost fun. Ambassador Marks had described the bizarre request for access to the alien technology that they imagined the US had in its possession. Carissa had told her about Rell's prank on Eileen, feeding her a load of bullshit about a super secret alien technology program, which Eileen had dutifully reported back to the Ministry of State Security. US intelligence had confirmed that Chinese leaders believed it, including Xi himself. Keala was going to have fun with it.

"President Xi, we were pleased to hear about your support for the international efforts in space, including the new treaty and your willingness to contribute to the removal of debris from our orbital neighborhood. We look forward to collaborating with you on these important global projects."

"We are happy to contribute our advanced technologies to the betterment of mankind and the peaceful uses of space, Madam President."

"That is good news indeed. Your country certainly possesses the ability to grab objects in space, as we have seen. Russia also has these capabilities, as do we. Would you be willing to coordinate the application of these satellite maintenance vehicles to the international effort?"

"Indeed, Madam President. Your timing is excellent. We are already preparing several launches of such maintenance vehicles and would happily coordinate with you and the Russians regarding the designation of specific areas of responsibility. As you know, we are capable of conducting a variety of operations in LEO, MEO and GEO."

"Yes, we are aware. I'm sure that you agree that the norms of behavior prohibiting aggression and the unjustified use of force here on Earth should be reflected in the space domain." She couldn't resist a subtle jab at Xi's sneak attack and his threats against Taiwan.

"Yes, we welcome such guidelines. Space belongs to all of us. I understand that our ambassadors in Geneva have already begun drafting treaty language. Our science advisors can exchange details about the coordinated actions, including any Russian or US advancements in Smoore Flow technology."

"Yes, of course, Mr. President. We will keep you fully informed about these promising developments."

Keala was enjoying her tactical advantage in keeping Xi guessing.

"Thank you, Madam President. These are promising developments for all mankind – or should I say all womankind as well. There is one other matter that merits attention."

Here it comes, she thought. Her NSC staff listening to the call were trying to suppress goofy grins.

"And what might that be, President Xi?"

"There are so many exciting discoveries in space, all of which carry tremendous implications for the people of Earth. Perhaps the most significant would be contact with alien species, especially if such extraterrestrial forces explain the confusion we have experienced. Don't you agree?"

"Yes, I agree. Contact with alien species would have tremendous consequences for all of us."

She was going to make him say it.

"Madam President, it would seem that such contacts would fit naturally into the cooperative efforts that you have so insightfully proposed. Wouldn't you agree?"

He was trying to hem her in with a logical trap.

"I agree wholeheartedly that contact with alien species would warrant a high degree of international cooperation to assess potential threats -- and opportunities."

She was glad this wasn't a video call because she was giggling now.

"If any country had information about such contacts, would it not make sense to share it? We should include this topic in the new treaty. I can assure you that we would share such information with you in the spirit of international cooperation."

"Mr. President, do you have such information?"

"Nothing concrete, but we have had indications that your government may be in possession of some physical specimens related to this topic. Perhaps we could exchange information for joint research under the provisions for planetary defense, which our representatives in Geneva have already outlined in the draft treaty."

"That is an excellent idea, Mr. President. I will consult with my science advisors, and we will follow up with suggestions for joint research. I assume you will also coordinate with Moscow. I am sure that you share my enthusiasm for using this crisis as a starting point for improved relations and economic prosperity."

"We, too, are excited about the prospects for peace and security. Thank you, President Kennelly, for your leadership in these matters."

"Thank you, President Xi, for your bold vision. You will hear from us shortly."

As the call ended, Keala and her advisors who were gathered in the White House, were almost in tears with laughter. "We should give them something!" the National Security Advisor offered. "Yeah, from the secret vault in Area 51!" guffawed NSC space policy guru Lisa Owens. "Ambassador Marks thinks they're watching X-Files reruns on the SyFy channel, or Ancient Aliens," added the Secretary of State. "Or maybe just Congressional UFO hearings," added the President. "What did you think, Carissa?"

Still unsure about her policy role, Carissa was hesitant to join the merriment. "From a technical perspective..." The President cut her off mid-sentence. "No, I want your overall judgment, Carissa. What should we do?" She straightened in her chair.

"I think it would be fun to give them bogus alien parts, you know, from the secret vault. I suspect they are after DNA samples that they can put into their DNA database, along with all the genetic information they are gathering from hacking Ancestry.com and 23 and Me. But I don't know how they might react when they figure out it's fake. They'll be mad, but it would be interesting to listen in on their conversations about extraterrestrial life forms, if we can put listening devices in the fake stuff. I'm not sure, however, how much that gets us. The bigger picture is how this all fits together – the orbital clean-up, the Chinese, the Russians, the Indians, our allies, international cooperation, the treaty, the new satellite infrastructure, and what it all means for the world. I think we need a strategy."

There was a long silence, with all eyes boring down on Carissa, who was already regretting speaking up. But it was too late to take it back, so she continued. "What we do in space could open opportunities to address all kinds of problems here on Earth, like poverty and climate change. We have to do it anyway, so why not use space to reshape the way we do things? Sorry, I'm just a scientist and..." "That's why you're here,

Carissa. We do need a strategy. And you're going to write it." Oh god, what had she gotten herself into? This was George's fault, all these big ideas. "Can I pick the team?" she asked. "Yes, but I have some suggestions for people who can really help you."

The President ordered her CIA Director to review options for giving Beijing fake alien technology, then said, "Let's do the call with Putin and get it over with. What an ass. Carissa, what do we say about the Flow? Do we offer them a joint research program?"

"I suppose it wouldn't hurt, it wouldn't cost us anything, and we might get something out of it. We already have the data, but they're already back doing experiments in space to characterize the energy transport mechanisms. That could be helpful. Plus, we're doing our experiments now. We could also consider a big international study using the ISS. My friend Lucky Slater, who helped design Quicksilver, is building his private space station. We might be able to use that, too, for an international research program."

"All right, I want the NASA Administrator to get me a plan for international research on this Flow stuff. Lisa, can you get that going?"

"Yes, Madam President. I'll round up the usual suspects. I assume we want the private sector involved?"

"Yes, it's time to pull them back in. OK, let's talk to Comrade Putin. Have you all seen the intelligence reporting on Kremlin rumors that his old KGB buddies are planning to exterminate him? Would it make sense for us to amplify those rumors? Poor Vladimir must be losing his shit."

The staff made a secure connection with the Russian leader, who was in the bathtub. Thankfully, it was not a video call.

"Dear Madam President, I was expecting your call. We have many things to discuss."

"Yes, Vladimir, we were happy to see that you called off another ill-advised invasion of Ukraine. Another serious miscalculation could have dire consequences. Looking to the future, I was encouraged by your receptivity to a collaborative approach to the orbital debris and your openness to combined research. We have a big job ahead of us."

She could hear splashing in the bathtub but tried not to think about the disgusting image of the Russian leader scrubbing his nether regions.

"I wanted to speak with you about such things, Ke-Allah. Is that how you say it? Key-Allah, like the Muslim god?"

"Yes, Vlad, that's almost correct. I understand your space force is preparing to remove debris from orbit. Will you be using the Flower Blossom on-orbit servicing units, the ones from the Chinese moon base?" She knew this would get his goat.

"Actually, Ke-Allah, the moon base is ours. However, we have agreed to lease it to our Chinese colleagues for scientific purposes. But your information is correct that we are preparing to use our advanced space capabilities to restore the sanctity of orbital freedoms. We would, of course, welcome American participation. Perhaps you might learn something." More splashing in the background. Yuk.

"Yes, Vlad, that is precisely what I had in mind. Do you think we might coordinate our orbital remediation efforts, perhaps in line with the treaty norms that our ambassadors are drafting in Geneva? Your friends in Beijing have already agreed." Yes, you bastard, she thought to herself, I called them first.

"Ke-Allah, we share many vital interests in space. We have recently discovered interesting new phenomena that may offer additional avenues for cooperation. We are working on ways to use such discoveries for the betterment of all mankind. Inshallah, as our Arab friends like to say. God willing. Is that an Islamic name, Ke-Allah?"

"No, Vlad, it's Irish. We agree, then, to move forward on the coordinated clean-up and the treaty. We should design some joint experiments for the International Space Station. I will have my science advisor contact your office regarding joint research on the Smoore Flow. I presume that is the new phenomena that you are alluding to."

"Ahh, you understand. Good. I have heard that you have excellent scientific advisors to help you understand such complex matters. However, as the discoverers of the new phenomenon, we have named it the Wasileski Effect to honor the brilliant Russian scientist who discovered it. I believe you know of him. That reminds me; have you considered our proposal to exchange knowledge about the new phenomena for immediate relief from the sanctions that you so frivolously imposed upon us? I assure you that treating us with respect is the surest path to the new world order that we all envision."

She wasn't taking the bait.

"Then we agree on moving ahead with the multinational clean-up campaign and the new treaty on space governance, which we believe heralds the beginning of an exciting new era for all our nations. We look forward to working with Russia on a wide range of research and development. It has been a pleasure speaking with you, Vladimir. Goodbye."

Keala took a few deep yoga breaths to calm herself and thought, "Carissa does yoga. I should ask her about meditation and breath control. I need to relax."

She turned to her staff and said, "What a piece of shit that guy is. Was he really in the bathtub? Disgusting. It doesn't matter. Our plans are coming together. We don't need the Russians to rebuild the global economy. John McCain was right. They're nothing more than a gas station masquerading as a country. I miss that guy, John McCain. We have a ton of work to do. Are the Nationals playing tonight?"

CHAPTER THIRTY

Dharma Bums

With the Chinese on board and the Russians negotiating, the President and her advisors needed to figure out how to involve the other space-faring nations in their plans. Everyone had a dog in this fight. Japan, South Korea, Australia, and all the NATO countries could be counted on to contribute. Israel, as well. Other countries might need additional incentives, like access to the replacement navigation systems and free internet. But what about India?

The Indian Space Research Organization has made great strides in designing, launching and operating satellites for military, intelligence and economic purposes. They had sent several manned missions to the moon and had established a moon base to stake their claim on lunar resources. India was a major player in the new space race, and they were ready to compete for their share of the new economy. Delhi's ties to Moscow, however, and its sanctions-busting behavior that provided Russia with desperately needed cash interfered with American hopes to foster a genuine alliance between the world's largest democracies. India was important as a counterbalance to China and a key member of the Quad, but Modi was still insisting on India's special status as a non-aligned nation, free to seek advantages wherever it chose. They had already made it clear that India would sit out any defense of Taiwan. Where would it fit in the new world order that was arising in the aftermath of the celestial demolition derby? India had lost almost all of its satellites and needed to rebuild, like everyone else. Would Prime Minister Modi agree to cooperate or insist on going his own way? Keala needed to find out.

"Prime Minister Modi, it's so nice to speak with you."

"It's always a pleasure to speak with you, Madam President."

"Call me Keala. May I call you Narendra?"

"If you must."

"As you wish, Mr. Prime Minister. Congratulations on your re-election."

"Thank you, Keala. And how may I help you?"

So that's how it is? He can call me by my first name, and yet he prefers that I address him formally. What a dick. No friendly chit-chat. Fine. Straight to business.

"Mr. Prime Minister, we have all suffered from the unfortunate events in space. Like all of us, you have lost your space-based navigation system, and your economy has been set back significantly."

"We are not as bad off as you may think, Keala. We Indians are resilient and resourceful. Our culture is rooted in thousands of years of Hindu tradition. A few satellites will not determine our destiny. We are not so dependent on technology as you are. Perhaps we should thank you for denying us access to technology because we are self-sufficient without it."

"We certainly appreciate how proud you are of your cultural heritage, Mr. Prime Minister. What I wanted to discuss with you today is the prospect of cooperating on the reestablishment of a peaceful space environment. Our two countries possess tremendous capacity to...."

He cut her off mid-sentence.

"Yes, yes, we are a leading space power, and we will be increasingly dominant in all matters of science and technology, including space. We are on the moon and shall lead the way to Mars. Our scientists are pushing back the frontiers of knowledge in every field imaginable. Gone are the days when America and the West can dictate the content and direction of knowledge itself. A new day has dawned, Keala. It's time you accepted it."

Keala closed her eyes and took a deep breath. Why did he insist on being so difficult?

"That's exactly what I wanted to speak with you about, Mr. Prime Minister. As you have noted, your growing status in the world puts you in an ideal position to shape how space is used to serve all of humanity. It would be only natural for India to take the lead in drafting a multilateral treaty on the governance of space. In this regard, we would look favorably at India's longstanding interest in becoming a permanent member of the United Nations Security Council. And we would like to collaborate with you on the clean-up and reimagining of the space domain. It is, as you say, the dawn of a new era.

We look forward to working with you on all of these important matters."

"President Kennelly, it is important for you to understand that we are not asking for your permission. We are demanding what is rightfully ours. Our recent victory over the Chinese should make it abundantly clear that India has claimed its rightful place as a great power. This is simply a fact that the world must accept."

It was quite an exaggeration to call the Himalayan standoff a victory, but Keala was looking for an angle to draw him in. She just needed India to join the treaty negotiation, help with the clean-up, and not play the role of spoiler by rallying opposition to the treaty among a bunch of disaffected nations, especially the BRICS – the oddball grouping of Brazil, Russia, India, China, and South Africa.

She assumed that bad actors such as Iran, North Korea, Syria, Venezuela, and a few others would always find ways to make trouble. But, according to Carissa, Indian scientists were already integrated throughout the international scientific community and were eager to collaborate on all sorts of space research and development, including the Smoore Flow phenomena. It would be nice if India would come on board as a true ally, but for now the President just needed Modi to go along with the program. It was fine if he wanted to claim credit. So much the better.

"I perfectly understand, Mr. Prime Minister. Congratulations on your reelection, and I look forward to continued cooperation between our two great democracies. Thank you for your time."

Ending the call, Keala turned to her NSC staff. "He just can't take yes for an answer, can he?"

Modi immediately called Putin. "Vladimir, what the hell is this American treaty? You're not going to sign it, are you?"

"Don't worry about it, Narendra. The Americans love these treaties. It makes them feel good, like Jesus Christ and Bill Gates are running the world. It costs us nothing."

"I want them to accept the new order, Vladimir. Jesus and Bill Gates are not running the world! Not anymore, at least. They need to accept the new reality. Their time has passed. It's our turn now."

"You're right, Narendra. Jesus and Bill Gates are not running the world, but it does not harm to let them think that they are, at least for a while. Let us indulge them in their capitalist delusions while their power drains away and the new world emerges around them, like the frog in a pot who does not recognize danger until it is too late. It will come as a delicious surprise when they awaken and find they have been cut down to size. Be patient, my friend."

"And what about this space business, with you and the Chinese? You didn't tell me about Flower Blossom and the moon base. We are on the moon too, don't forget. And we found water before any of you. But the Chinese attacked our satellites. How can we trust them?"

"You don't have to trust them, Narendra. We just have to present a united front against the Americans. Their allies will abandon them like rats on a sinking ship, and the poor countries will see through their hypocrisy. Remember the old Russian saying: the enemy of my enemy is my friend."

"I thought that was a French saying or Arabic, but it doesn't matter. Should we convene a meeting of the BRICS or the SCO to offer an alternative to the American's plans?"

"I don't think it is necessary. It might just slow things down. We are already managing the Americans' bid to dominate the future. Together, we are stronger. Our time is coming. Be patient."

"Can you control Xi's lust for power? We respect your right to a buffer zone with NATO, and we could care less about Taiwan, but we will not tolerate Chinese aggression against our borders. How do we counterbalance American power if China does not respect our territorial integrity? Their Pakistani proxies continue to threaten our security. Have you seen how many nuclear weapons they have? It's really quite alarming."

"Calm down, Narendra. The Pakistanis aren't going to attack you with nuclear weapons. I'll talk to Xi. The West is to blame for your border woes, but it is a sideshow. The American century is over. They just don't know it yet."

"Thank you, Vladimir. You are a true friend. We will accept the American proposals for space cooperation, for now. Please talk to Xi. We will stand together."

Putin called Xi to discuss the next steps. They needed to prevent India from siding with the Americans. Xi and Putin were still convinced that

America and the West were on the slippery slope of imperial overreach, teetering on the edge of cataclysmic social decay and paying the price for trying to be the world's policeman. Appealing to India's deeply ingrained anti-colonial sentiments, it was not difficult to play the India card against the US with offers of discounted weapons sales and cheap, sanctions-busting oil. And, despite their longstanding hatred, Sino-Indian trade continued to grow. Let Modi think he is the master of the game, flirting with Washington while sleeping with us.

"Mr Putin, to what do I owe the honor of speaking with you?"

It was difficult for Xi to hide his antipathy for the Russian leader, but he needed him for now.

"Chairman Xi, it is indeed a pleasure to speak with you. I would like to discuss our friend in Delhi. He is nervous about the American space plans. He may need a nudge if you know what I mean."

"A nudge? Do you mean toward an open window? I thought that was your specialty for dealing with recalcitrant colleagues. I don't do windows."

"Very funny, my friend. But what I have in mind is more carrot than stick, at least for now. The Americans and their allies are moving quickly to repopulate the orbits. NATO, the European Space Agency, Japan, Korea, and Australia are all getting into the act. Others too. Perhaps it is time to offer an alternative to the capitalist model. Many countries in Africa and Latin America would be sympathetic to a different narrative if it were properly cultivated. What would you think about a BRICS or Shanghai Cooperation Organization (SCO) meeting on the future of space, where we characterize the American-led efforts and the stupid treaty they are foisting on us as nothing more than the latest expression of neo-colonial exploitation? The Indians would eat it up."

"Vladimir, I must be reminded never to underestimate your cunning. That is an excellent idea. The alternative model you suggest could be incentivized by subsidized access to our space technologies, which will then bind the recipient countries to us, as the Huawei telecommunications equipment did for our Belt-Road Initiative. The new Beido navigation network will become their guiding light and ours. Our satellites will control the new economy. We have been planning to propose a new currency to replace the dollar. This might be the right time to help finance the new space services. Don't worry, Vlad, we will give you some great deals.

"We may need help financing the new GLOSNASS network."

"Of course. No problem. Your oil will secure the loans. Does Modi want to host the meeting in India, or does he prefer a cutout to avoid the wrath of the Americans, who think they have this all figured out already? BRICS or SCO?"

"I think a cutout is in order. Perhaps Brazil or South Africa so that it would be the BRICS. I would suggest Pakistan, but that would drive the Indians crazy – more than usual."

"I must admit, I derive some satisfaction from driving the Indians crazy. It's not difficult to do. Let us plan for a meeting of the BRICS in Rio de Janeiro, where we will unveil the people's alternative for space governance in the new world order. And Vladimir, stay away from windows."

CHAPTER THIRTY ONE

Space Is the Place

The Afro-futurist jazz artist Sun Ra predicted in 1972 that "space is the place." Operation Clean Sweep, as it was called, sparked a renaissance of space R&D, with innovative new launch technologies and satellite designs being developed at a breakneck pace. The US, Russia, China, Europe, and India started launching satellites on a daily basis. Their tow truck satellites grabbed chunks of debris and corralled them into designated quarantine zones, like cowboys herding cattle. Scientists around the world have devised new ways to permanently dispose of the collected trash piles, clearing the way for new satellites. Some of the larger pieces could be safely de-orbited and either burn up in the atmosphere or crash down harmlessly in remote areas of the Earth's surface. The odds of landing in populated areas were infinitesimally small.

Still, rumors spread of a deadly "vaccine rain" being produced by a mysterious global conspiracy led by Bill Gates, Bono, and Barak Obama. According to Q Anon Plus followers, the space debris had been impregnated with race-specific agents that were produced on the International Space Station. The phony space war was all a pretense to disseminate a "vaccine" that was designed to sterilize Caucasians and expedite their replacement by Jews and blacks. News Max, Breitbart and the Epoch Times ran the story, and it was soon picked up by members of Congress who spouted it on Fox News. "I'm not saying we know for sure what's really going on up there, but it certainly bears looking into," said one conspiracy-prone member. "Where there's smoke, there's fire," said another blithely. The chairman of a prominent House committee proclaimed, "When you add this information to the disturbing testimony about undisclosed alien technology, we would be irresponsible not to investigate. We plan to hold hearings." The lack of evidence for any of it did not matter.

Many pieces of debris could be physically pushed outward by the self-propelled clean-up bots beyond the reach of Earth's gravity and were dispatched into deep space. The Russian and Chinese space agencies used their murder hornet satellites to sling some of the larger chunks out of Earth orbit into the solar system, while the US Space Force employed its Quicksilver class of maneuvering satellites to tow away and bundle the trash in its areas of responsibility. All three countries, plus India, experimented with using lasers to disintegrate the smaller particles, using their ground and space-based ASAT options. Defensive weapons, of course, would not be banned by the new treaty.

In the spirit of cooperation, the four leading space nations concentrated their high-power lasers on agreed targets to incinerate some of the more stubborn pieces of debris. Their combined power levels, timing, angles of attack, and coordinated frequencies enabled the laser teams to widen the focal point to eliminate concentrations of debris, like a kid burning ants with a magnifying glass. The combined laser power improved efficiency by zapping bigger areas rather than focusing on individual chunks of debris, one at a time. It didn't matter that all four countries were using the opportunity to improve their laser ASAT capabilities. For now, incinerating objects in space serves a good cause.

Carissa's team at Livermore supported the clean-up operations with real-time target selection and traffic management for the surge of launches and intensified satellite activity. Duke was working overtime to keep pace. Oppie mapped the dwindling radiation fields. The team enjoyed the daily video-link collaboration with their Russian, Chinese, and Indian counterparts and the sharing of data from the fast-growing network of optics and sensors. Operation Clean Sweep made excellent progress, especially in LEO, where most of the debris was concentrated. At the operational levels, scientists and military operators embraced international cooperation to get the job done. In Geneva, diplomats were close to completing the new draft space treaty. The new era had begun.

In the Livermore command center, Rell Sunn doubled down on their pranks. On a video call with the Russians, Chinese, and Indians, Rell pretended to cover the microphone before leaning over and conspicuously confiding to Eileen that "the secret alien technology would be perfect for Clean Sweep if only they would let us talk about it." They put up pictures of aliens in their work area, adjacent to the op center, just visible on the edge of the camera range on the video broadcasts. Chinese intelligence officers joined the calls to watch Rell and Eileen, who were still not in on the joke.

The Chinese asked the Russians, who asked the Indians, about evidence that the Americans had made first contact with alien life forms. Rell's feigned breach of secret information seemed to confirm Congressional testimony from former intelligence officers who claimed to know about a secret stash of alien "biologics." What Rell did not know was that the CIA's S&T directorate had constructed a variety of bogus alien artifacts to share with the Chinese if the President authorized the alien technology hoax. The agency was also still trying to decide if Eileen should hand over the goods as if she had stolen them from the secret vault or make it part of an official exchange. "What else are they hiding?" Xi asked his advisors. "What if they have a super weapon?" mused Putin. "It should have been us if not for Colonial oppression." raged Modi.

The real unexplained phenomena, however, was not alien life forms, but how to use the Smoore Flow to transport debris via the rivers of energy that they now knew existed. Livermore's Stellar Occultation

Hypertemporal Imaging telescope on the ISS had mapped the energy flows, and Gerry Lopez and his team at Los Alamos lab had entered the new data into Oppie, the ultra-high performance computer program that modeled electromagnetic energies in space. When combined with Andrei's experimental data from the Russian space sensors (which the National Security Agency had successfully hacked), the results were astonishing. Photos showed swirling eddies of subatomic particles, not unlike the Northern Lights, flowing outward through LEO, MEO and GEO, reminiscent of the awe-inspiring photos of the universe from the Webb Telescope before the scorched skies ruined it.

The Smoore Flow lit up the heavens with green, purple, and orange undulating fluorescent flames, like jellyfish tentacles or a gently swaying psychedelic kelp forest. Garrett McNamara said it reminded him of the flames painted on the gas tank of his Harley. Now that they could see them, the big question was how to direct the Flow to sweep any remaining debris out of Earth's orbit toward the vast emptiness of the solar system. Could you surf the Flow waves like the Silver Surfer shredding the universe? How far did the waves go? Nobody knew. The scientists were thrilled and happy to work together to understand the new phenomena, no matter who discovered it.

Many countries wanted to contribute to Clean Sweep. Japan and South Korea used the joint space program that they had forged to combat North Korea's nuclear, missile and space weapons to track and destroy some of the space debris. It was also useful target practice for their missile defenses against North Korean and Chinese missiles. NATO devoted its combined missile defenses to supporting Clean Sweep while designing its new navigation and communications systems for the Alliance, including a dedicated nuclear command and control and communications (NC3) infrastructure to reinforce deterrence. The European Space Agency unveiled an ambitious replacement satellite program to support climate science, food security, and disaster assistance. The new space architecture was coming into focus, but instead of following an overall design, nations, agencies, alliances, and companies were all rushing to fill the void as fast as possible. Nobody knew what the outcome would look like.

The Russians, Chinese and Indians were right that the space renaissance would facilitate the emergence of a new world order, but it was not exactly how they had imagined it. In the Middle East, Israel, Jordan, Saudi Arabia, UAE, Turkey, and Egypt formed a new space coalition to launch and operate a regional navigation and communications network. An Arctic alliance of Canada, the US, Greenland (Denmark), Iceland, Finland, Norway, and Sweden deployed a dedicated satellite network to track developments in the far North, and Argentina, Chile, Australia, New Zealand, and South Africa formed an equivalent network for Antarctica. Indonesia organized a new Pacific Space Alliance under the ASEAN banner, and in Africa, several new groups formed to develop satellite networks for the northern, central and southern regions of the Continent. The BRICS space alliance would have plenty of competition. Space was quickly becoming as crowded, congested, and contested as it was before the Kessler Effect wiped out the first space age. The new world of space alliances resembled a kaleidoscope of shifting patterns, with old friends and strange bedfellows teaming up to reinvent the space domain.

The new space race ignited a voracious demand for space technologies. Investors channeled trillions of dollars into the burgeoning space economy that was realigning the global balance of power. Launch centers sprung to life across the globe, sprouting new generations of big and small rockets as well as a panoply of innovative launch methods to hurl payloads into orbit using slings, rail guns and cannons. New means of propulsion and guidance concepts prepared to meet the demand. Constellations of cube sats would incorporate a staggering array of emerging technologies, including advanced materials, chips, microelectronics, production methods, quantum clocks, quantum communications, and blockchain technologies to protect them from hackers. Powerful optics and sensors would provide persistent surveillance of every inch of Earth's surface, adding oceans of data to be analyzed with petaflop computers, artificial intelligence, and machine learning algorithms. Integrated edge computing would guide swarms of maneuverable cube sats in every imaginable orbit to gather information from every frequency on the electromagnetic spectrum about the atmospheric, oceanic, terrestrial, sub-terrestrial and human domains. The latter would raise questions about privacy since the new optics and sensors could identify and track any person or anything, any time, any place on Earth. Watch out, critics warned, here comes the Brave New World. Big Brother is coming! But first, Operation Clean Sweep would have to set the stage for the second space age.

New companies and old paragons of industry surged to provide the technologies and services for the space renaissance. The money was free-flowing as governments offered incentives to expedite ossified procurement processes, originally intended to oversee contracts, guarantee quality, and minimize corruption, but now blocking governments from keeping pace with the private sector. The new space economy was starting more like the Wild West than a planned community. Everything was happening fast. Scientists, spies, warfighters and entrepreneurs were ready to feast on the banquet of data from the supercharged satellite infrastructure. Lucky Slater relished the demand for his Malibu space station, on which he planned to realize his dream of living in space. He had already designed a space suit for himself and one for his dog, Dora. The outlook for space travel had never been better.

Carissa, who had agreed to produce a space strategy document for the President, was learning some hard lessons. Nobody was waiting around for the government's plan. Her group of respected experts met weekly under the auspices of the White House Office of Science and Technology Policy. They were making progress outlining how the emerging space economy could revolutionize every aspect of domestic and international security as George had imagined. But as the weeks passed, so did the opportunity to offer a coordinated strategy. The new reality was coming together faster than the government strategy. How was this barely regulated free market going to achieve the ambitious goals? What about George's ideas about using the opportunity to solve big problems like poverty and climate change? Carissa wanted to move at the speed of relevance, but the government could not keep up. She was also getting tired of the weekly flights back and forth between Washington and California. It was lonely. Being the President's science advisor was hard.

CHAPTER THIRTY-TWO

Harvest for the World

As the Sino-Indian border war fizzled, the troops went home, and Putin and Xi shelved their plans to invade their neighbors – for now. India proclaimed victory "on land, at sea, and in the cosmos." The media bounced from the Himalayan war to the space catastrophe, to the economic meltdown, to the emergence of a new world order, to the next headline. The world mostly settled into a period of national introspection, focused on economic growth and domestic renewal. The burgeoning space economy brought unimagined opportunities, with capital flowing and new companies offering a dizzying array of previously unimaginable technologies and services. International commerce would never be the same, with revolutionary changes in the banking, transportation, and manufacturing sectors driving new business models.

Lucky Slater's modular Malibu space stations were a good example of the economic changes. His space space-based, zero-gravity manufacturing stations started with pharmaceuticals and quickly expanded to 3D printing microelectronics using super-conductive materials that were impossible to work with on Earth. Malibu 2 would make next-generation rechargeable batteries. Malibu 3 would make human eyeballs. The financing for his space stations came from an American Indian tribe that owned casinos and was also interested in the prospects for casinos in space. "The sky's no limit," Lucky told them.

Lucky soon realized his dream of space travel, traveling with his dog Dora in a SpaceX delivery shuttle to survey the Malibu 1 manufacturing facility. They were able to stay in Malibu for a week before returning home. Dora never regained her sense of balance, so Lucky moved off his boat into a house in Laurel Canyon that was formerly owned by sci-fi godfather Ray Bradbury. Dora was grateful to be on solid ground, but Lucky was planning his next trip, this time to Malibu 2.

Reny Yater spun off his own company to track and maintain satellites for government and private clients. He hired Jeff Clark, Laird Hamilton and Jake Burton away from the Space Force to run his network of tracking stations, doubling their government salaries, with the understanding that they would not be required to move away from their beloved surfing and skiing havens. Yater tried to lure Carissa away from the lab, but even the offer to triple her salary was not enough to overcome her love of science and her affection for her team at Livermore. He had to settle for Garrett McNamara and his wife, who were expecting their first child and starting to think about paying for college. They would help run Yater's new space traffic management control center, which he was building on the central California coast near San Luis Obispo.

On-orbit fueling and satellite maintenance services were becoming routine. Asteroid mining was suddenly within reach, and moon bases were sprouting like tulips in spring. Trips to and from the moon were becoming a daily occurrence. Closer to Earth, high-altitude flight, hypersonic aircraft, and routine access to Very Low Earth Orbit (VLEO, below 250 miles) revolutionized air travel. Even the Baby Boomers' long-desired flying cars were becoming a reality, although the Transportation Department, the FAA, the TSA and the insurance companies would struggle to keep pace with the increasingly crowded and contested skies. Fortunately, quantum-powered, AI accelerated navigational decision making would help to avoid collisions. The revolution in transportation and delivery had begun.

With so many innovations happening at once, many of the ideological goals outlined in Carissa and George's strategy were becoming reality.

Every place on Earth would have access to the internet, with secure and instantaneous data streams available to all. Space-based solar collectors would stream clean energy to whoever needed it for a reasonable cost, lowering fossil fuel emissions and making a huge dent in the climate crisis. The new generation of ubiquitous and unhackable navigation services combined with quantum computing opened the gates to a new era in autonomous vehicles of all types, on land, sea and in the air. Clearing out the old space infrastructure had opened the floodgates to the Fourth Industrial Age.

The new space architecture was bigger, better, faster, cheaper, and more democratic because it opened space to nearly anyone and was no longer the exclusive providence of a few rich and powerful nations, organizations, or individuals. Accelerating the pace of change, a new generation of leaders was quicker to adopt innovative technologies and business practices, and they wasted no time with antiquated notions about race, gender, or sexual orientation. White supremacy and male chauvinism shriveled and died, not due to laws, but because events simply overtook them. Diversity and human capital became essential ingredients for success, and everybody knew it. The expansion of the human talent pool accelerated everything. The reimagined space economy, however, did not alter human nature. Criminals quickly adapted the new technologies to lie, cheat and steal, and law enforcement agencies were equally motivated to enlist the new technologies to track and prosecute them. From that perspective, nothing changed.

Most nations welcomed the Artemis space treaty, with its provisions for space commerce, orbital traffic management, cyber security, liability, and restrictions on military activities. The strong prohibitions against the stationing or manufacture of weapons of mass destruction in space were particularly popular, although nobody could agree on what constitutes WMD in space, so the definitions remained frustratingly vague. What new weapons might be possible in space? Was the Kessler Effect a weapon of mass destruction? What about the Smoore Flow, if it could be weaponized? The treaty negotiators established a working group to examine those issues.

Truthfully, the new treaty simply combined the five already existing space treaties -The Outer Space Treaty, the Liability Convention, the Moon Agreement, the Rescue and Return Agreement, and the Registration Convention – into a single, overarching covenant for space governance. The big victory for US diplomats was overcoming Russian and Chinese opposition to calling the umbrella document the Artemis Accords because it sounded like an extension of the American initiative, which it was.

Russia and China begrudgingly joined the Artemis Treaty but quickly lodged protests against Lucky Slater's pharmaceutical production space station as a cover for a secret US biological weapons program. As expected, negotiators could not agree on inspection, verification, or enforcement mechanisms. They did agree, however, to establish a new international organization for space governance (IOSG) based in Bangalore as part of a deal to get India to join. The Modi Center would quickly become a hotbed of international space research and development.

Russia, China, and India convened the BRICS to unveil what they hoped would be the alternative to Artemis and the rapidly expanding American coalitions, but without the bedrock reliability of the rule of law, investment capital shied away from authoritarian regimes, leaving the democracies in the driver's seat of the new economic order. China's ploy to replace the dollar with a universal cryptocurrency fell flat as investors demanded transparency and accountability. Better to stick with the devil you know than take unnecessary risks with the devil you don't know. Nobody trusted Xi or the PRC, much less Russia. The global banking and finance system had problems, but the alternatives were worse.

The corruption, shrinking economies and fateful demographic trends of both China and Russia forced Beijing and Moscow to self-fund their efforts to keep pace with the booming space economy. The Kessler Effect had wiped out their advantage. Russia's cheap oil and China's subsidized technology exports were no match for the entrepreneurs around the world who created innovative business models to connect emerging technologies with dynamic global markets. Why settle for subsidized, second-rate Huawei gear when you could have the latest and greatest technologies coming from Silicon Valley, Seoul, Europe, Bangalore, or the other emerging tech hubs around the world?

Even the new regional space alliances opted for team Artemis over Russia or China's state-owned, oligarch-controlled, second-rate technology firms. Cuba and Venezuela declined to participate in China's Belt and Road Initiative for Space and instead opted to join Brazil's new initiative to form a Southern Hemisphere Space Alliance. Iran, Turkey, Pakistan, Egypt, and the United Arab Emirates chose to buy American, Indian, and South Korean technologies rather than rely on China. Everyone still relied on computer chips made in Taiwan, Japan, South Korea and the US. The new geopolitical alignments had many familiar characteristics.

Isolated from the new space economy, Russia and China expanded their covert procurement networks to steal Western technologies, especially for their space programs. Without foreign investment, they simply could not compete. India grudgingly opened to foreign investment in its booming tech sector. With one foot in the global south and the other in the West, India offered an alternative to countries seeking a middle path between the authoritarian tyrants and the free market democracies. Only the truly desperate, like North Korea, Syria and

Myanmar, cast their lot with the Chinese and the Russians, taking help from wherever they could get it. Beggars can't be choosers.

CHAPTER THIRTY-THREE

Complex Deterrence and the Nth-Body Problem

In physics, the Nth body problem describes the difficulty of predicting the motions of more than two objects. This is particularly relevant for astrophysics, where multiple forces act on multiple objects. In strategic nuclear doctrine, the Nth body problem refers to the difficulty of predicting the actions of more than two nuclear-armed nations whose bilateral nuclear deterrence relationship is relatively stable and predictable. Adding a third or fourth country to the equation creates uncertainties about the complex deterrence relationships within the system.

The US-Soviet bipolar deterrence relationship was risky and complicated, but over time, both sides learned to avoid actions that might trigger a nuclear war. Events such as the Cuban Missile Crisis reinforced the importance of avoiding miscalculation. Adding China, North Korea, India, Pakistan and Iran to the mix of nuclear competitors greatly complicates the dynamics of deterrence because all these actors are interacting simultaneously. Further complicating matters, military competition in space adds new uncertainties, with nuclear command and control systems inextricably entwined with conventional military systems as well as commercial space activities. The space war demonstrated just how fragile the interconnected systems had become. The Kessler Effect had wiped it all out. Now, the space systems were being rebuilt, but the core problem of deterrence remained. Deterrence had become more complex and less predictable.

The President made complex, multi-domain deterrence her top priority. Space Command, Strategic Command, the other combatant commands, and the Joint Chiefs outlined their requirements. This was an opportunity to break with the past and make the leap into the future of warfare. That meant replacing large, vulnerable, and super expensive systems, like aircraft carriers and F-35 fighter jets, with swarms of agile, unmanned, expendable drones. Instead of the traditional stovepipes of forces operated by the Army, Navy, Air Force, and Marines, the new warfighting systems would be interconnected with a coordinated Joint All Domain Command and Control (JADAC2) system.

True interoperability was now possible due to the new space systems and the super-charged AI that would enable commanders to see the whole multi-domain battlefield and move agile forces to the most advantageous positions with maximum speed, precision, and lethality. Intelligence, Surveillance and Reconnaissance (ISR) would now extend from GEO, through LEO and VLOW, through the atmosphere, across the electromagnetic spectrum, over and under the oceans, and cover every inch of the Earth's surface. With such command of the battlefield, America's enemies would think twice before attacking. Added to this, advancements in missile defenses would make conventional deterrence stronger than ever. It wouldn't happen overnight, but at least the transition had begun.

At the strategic level, the President's plan called for a new generation of nuclear weapons and delivery systems to replace the aging Cold War arsenal. In contrast to the Russians and Chinese, who were pouring money into designing and deploying new generations of nuclear weapons and delivery systems, the US had simply maintained its old Cold War weapons, hoping the day would come when nuclear weapons no longer played a central role in the nation's defenses. Now, it was clear that deterrence required some upgrades. President Kennelly directed the national labs to design new warheads and delivery systems that would signal with maximum credibility that a WMD attack on the United States would be met with unbearable consequences. The new strategic triad would incorporate all of the emerging technologies and manufacturing techniques to ensure that the arsenal would remain safe, secure and reliable, with state-of-the-art nuclear command, control and communications (NC3).

The Department of Energy and its National Nuclear Security Administration would update its Cold War nuclear manufacturing facilities with advanced 3D printing machines capable of producing nuclear components using exotic new materials, including the plutonium and highly enriched uranium used to make nuclear weapon cores. Cheaper, faster, more reliable, and flexible, the new nuclear manufacturing capabilities would give the US the ability to ramp up production to meet changing circumstances and experiment with new concepts while guaranteeing safety, security and use control under every conceivable circumstance. The new space architecture would provide strategic warning of nuclear risks and give the President maximum options in a crisis. "Why didn't we do this earlier?" President Kennelly asked her National Security Council. Then, she directed her staff to draft a statement outlining America's contemporary nuclear deterrence strategy and posture. "I want the message to nuclear-armed adversaries to be crystal clear: If you fuck with the United States of America, you will rot on the ash heap of history. I guarantee it."

The President wanted to run her nuclear posture statement by her friend and science advisor, Dr. Carissa Moore.

"What do you think? Too much? I wanted to steal the Marine Corps motto, 'No better friend, no worse enemy,' but General Mattis told me the Marines wouldn't like it. I don't want to piss them off. Gotta love the Marines."

"Keala, this is way out of my league. I'm not a nuclear strategist, but my colleagues at the lab think about this stuff all day long. Can I run it by Dr. August at the Center for Global Security Research (CGSR)? He's a real deterrence expert. He wrote the previous nuclear posture review."

"Good idea, but please keep it quiet. Can he come to talk with me about it?"

"I'll ask him."

Dr. Robert August was the director of CGSR, the small think tank that was embedded inside Lawrence Livermore National Laboratory. Their job was to study the policy implications of technology, especially those related to nuclear weapons. August was a bear of a man, part learned scholar, part mountain man, with a reputation for straight talk. He would disappear for weeks in the Sierra backcountry, then crank out a torrent of books and articles before returning to the mountains. He had advised five presidents on nuclear strategy and policy. Sometimes, they even listened.

August sat with the President for two hours in the Oval Office, going over her statement about the new deterrence strategy. He described the importance of the arsenal being properly aligned with the mission, or "fit for purpose," and the need to strike the right balance between public fears of nuclear saber-rattling and clarity about the American response to nuclear aggression. The President asked him to explain how the pieces fit together – conventional, nuclear, cyber, and space deterrence.

"Do we need a separate deterrence strategy for every domain?"

"In theory, your deterrence posture should convey that we are prepared for any contingency. In practice, you need to back that up with specific, credible capabilities that are appropriate and proportional to the specific circumstances. This gets tricky with cyber and space, where the conflict may not be visible."

"Do we need a separate space deterrence policy?" she asked.

"The adversary must know with certainty that there will be unacceptable consequences for attacking our vital space assets. He or she must not believe that they can chip away at the margins and wear us down with a 'death by a thousand cuts' strategy. We call this the red theory of victory, where our enemies come close to our red lines and dare us to act, believing that we won't fight because the risks are too high. Since armed conflict in the space domain is relatively new, it may be necessary to state publicly the rules of the road – that at least some space assets are vital to our security and should be viewed as an extension of the homeland. The new space treaty lays out these norms, but it's probably prudent to state them explicitly in the context of your deterrence policy. You don't have to be specific about our response to aggression, but you need to let people know that you will respond in a way that will deny them any benefits."

"So, do we need a separate statement for space deterrence? That's how all this got started in the first place, with countries shooting at satellites. I want to make it clear that we will not stand by and allow this to happen again."

"It wouldn't have to be a stand-alone statement. It could be included with the broader upgraded deterrence policy."

"What about cyber? Do we need a separate statement for cyber deterrence?"

"It's even harder to be credible about our response to cyber attacks, especially if we are not at war because it's so embedded with civilian infrastructure. Deterrence works best when there is a prospect for a disproportional response, but we traditionally don't like to threaten attacks against civilian targets like hospitals and schools. I suppose we could say that we can retaliate selectively against military cyber targets."

"Okay. Dr. August, I'd like you to draft four statements. One on our overall deterrence posture, one on conventional deterrence, one on space deterrence, and one on cyber deterrence. One sentence each, Hemingway, not Gabriel Garcia Marquez. My staff will work them through the inter-agency process. Carissa, I know you're frustrated with the big space strategy, but I'd like you to sherpa this."

"Sherpa? I don't know what you mean. What's a sherpa?" Carissa said, perplexed.

"It means you make sure it gets done. Okay? Dr. August, we could use you in the Defense Department. Would you consider the Assistant Secretary for Policy position?"

"With all due respect, Madam President, I've been there and done that. I'm pretty happy where I am."

"Well, that's too bad, but you can't blame a girl for trying. Do you like baseball? Carissa and I are going to the Nats-Giants game tonight if you'd like to join us."

Dr. August drafted the four succinct statements, and Carissa sent them to the National Security Advisor, who initiated the inter-agency review process for the new integrated deterrence strategy. Predictably, the State Department wanted more diplomacy, the Defense Department wanted more weapons, the Intelligence Community wanted more spying, the Treasury Department wanted more sanctions, and the Commerce Department wanted more trade in the strategy. But the trailblazing document represented a true whole-of-government approach to the new world order, with America resuming its leadership of an expanding democratic alliance. Of course, the military services would fight to maintain their independence, and bureaucracies would haggle over their influence and resources, but at its core, the new deterrence strategy aligned with American strengths to prevent anyone from thinking they could threaten US security without suffering dire consequences.

CHAPTER THIRTY-FOUR

Spies Like US

The massive spike in space activities around the world presented numerous opportunities for spying. The CIA opened a new branch dedicated to collecting information about foreign space programs and recruited a new generation of space-savvy young case officers to steal secrets from America's adversaries. The National Security Agency developed a new lexicon for eavesdropping on space related conversations, and the FBI had a heyday tracking all the foreign spies trying to steal secrets from American companies. The National Geospatial Agency was awash with multi-spectral imagery from every corner of the globe. It was a good time for spies and spying.

At the National Reconnaissance Office, George Downing was working overtime designing the new space surveillance architecture. Replacing the damaged Silent Barker space surveillance network was the top priority, but Carissa had also roped him into helping her draft the White House grand strategy. They were both frustrated with the slow pace but happy to see their ideological ideas about using the space renaissance as a springboard to address other big problems, like climate change and food security. The experts appointed to the Presidential Commission on the New Global Space Economy mostly agreed on how space could be used to create a more just and prosperous society, but translating their meeting notes into a finished report, much less action, seemed to take forever. George and Carissa were both ready to get back to the work they loved. George was eager to focus on designing new satellites, and Carissa was chomping at the bit to dive into her research on the Smoore Flow, which somehow made her feel closer to her dad.

Eileen had become a double agent. She continued to pass information to her MSS handlers, but not before clearing it with the FBI counterintelligence officers assigned to her case. Gabriel Medina and Maya Gabiera worked out of the FBI's San Francisco office, mostly tracking Chinese espionage in Silicon Valley. Medina was from the FBI's WMD Division. He grew up in LA, joined the Army, and trained to become a specialist in chemical and biological weapons. His partner Maya Gabiera immigrated with her family from Brazil as a child, earned her law degree from Tulane and joined the FBI after a stint as a district attorney in Baton Rouge. Their territory included Lawrence Livermore and Lawrence Berkeley Labs because both were major targets for foreign agents trying to steal American technology.

After talking with Rell about her alien pranks on Eileen, Gabiera and Medina came up with a plan. They were impressed but also a little shocked by Rell's ruthlessness in exploiting Eileen's gullibility and her enthusiasm for continuing the ruse. Rell wanted to keep Eileen in the dark and use her to pass along all sorts of phony documents, including falsified nuclear secrets, to the Chinese. "We can fuck up their nuclear program by feeding them doctored diagnostic codes," Rell told the FBI agents. The FBI vetoed that approach and decided instead to level with Eileen in exchange for her cooperation. She would be more useful as a writing accomplice, especially if they promised her asylum and the prospect of US citizenship. All she had to do was keep texting her MSS handlers. They would provide her with information to pass along.

As counterintelligence officers, Maya and Gabriel tracked Chinese agents and tried to locate the sources of leaks of classified information. They wanted to give traceable information to Eileen and see where it went inside the Chinese spy network. It might reveal other spies. Maya and Gabriel wanted Rell to give Eileen bogus information about FBI surveillance and counterintelligence around Bay Area labs and tech firms to see how the MSS adjusted their operations.

The CIA, however, had a different idea. Patty, who had run the exfiltration of Andrei from India, and her team wanted Eileen to pass their counterfeit alien technology to the MSS. The operation would require a physical meeting rather than just texting, which would draw the MSS into the open. The FBI could still track the Chinese agents, but the CIA could also track the counterfeit items to see where the MSS took them, who worked on them, and what methods the Chinese scientists used to decipher the mystery. Covert tracking devices woven into the alien gizmos would provide valuable information about China's classified R&D labs. Eileen would still get asylum.

The President had discussed it with Carissa and had authorized the operation, with a promise that Eileen would keep her job at the Lab and Rell would be read into the operation. If and when the Chinese experts discovered the truth, they were more likely to cover it up than turn it into an international incident. Better to let them think they stole the items than offer them as part of an official scientific exchange. The benefits outweighed the risks.

Eileen agreed to tell the MSS that she had important items to give them but would need to meet in person. Rell loved the whole idea and volunteered to provide the alien widgets to Eileen as part of the operation. One question remained: Should they tell Eileen the truth about the artifacts or let her continue to think they were real? "We can tell her after it's over," Rell advised Patty and her CIA operatives. "What's the benefit of telling her now? It'll just freak her out." Patty exclaimed, "Man, I love this chick, or this they, or whatever they want to be called. Carissa, your whole team is fantastic, a den of natural spies. I mean that as a compliment. Rell's right. We won't tell Eileen until it's over." They would tell Eileen everything except that the alien technology was bullshit.

Eileen texted her MSS handlers and told them she had acquired samples of the alien technology from Rell, who supposedly worked on the program and had left them on her desk – the same desk that the MSS had been watching on the edge of the video conferences. She needed to meet in person to pass them along, and it would have to be in the Bay Area. The MSS agreed to the meet-up and gave her instructions to meet their contact in Alameda at the USS Hornet.

The Hornet is a famous World War Two aircraft carrier that has become a floating museum at the old Alameda Point Naval Air Station. Eileen would board the Hornet and meet her contact in front of the Airstream trailer that had served as the contamination confinement unit for the Apollo 11 astronauts when the Hornet retrieved them after their mission to the moon, with President Nixon on board to greet them. "How ironic is that? They want to meet on the Hornet," Carissa mused. "Do you think they're sending us a message?"

The CIA had used 3D printing to produce an unlikely meta-material concocted of beryllium, titanium, and graphene. They programmed the printer to produce an impossibly shaped object, riddled with intricate, swirling internal lattices and laced with polymers that also served as covert antennae that would allow the agency to track its whereabouts. The mysterious object resembled an MC Esher creation, with folds and flanges that made no sense. It was about four inches long and three inches wide, platinum gray in color, with slightly rounded edges, uneven surfaces and irregular contours. After a long argument about taking the joke too far, the CIA machinists added a sexually explicit, microscopic emblem that they copied from an ancient Egyptian rune. Then they burned, pressure treated, sandblasted, electrified, magnetized, and partially crushed it, so it looked like it could have travelled across the universe and crashed into the Mojave Desert. The result was a gray metallic, slightly oblong component that would fit in the palm of your hand. They wanted it to look like it was supposed to fit into some larger piece of extraterrestrial equipment. For DNA traces, they smeared it with octopus slime. "This should freak them out," the CIA science and technology team concluded.

Eileen would deliver the orb to the Hornet in a plastic bag. She would tell her to contact that she stole it from a box on Rell's desk, which was conspicuously visible but tantalizingly out of the field of vision during the recent international Clean Sweep video conferences a few days before the hand-off. They knew the MSS was closely monitoring the video sessions, searching for any information about the lab and its people. Eileen would text the MSS that there were other objects in the wooden box on Rell's desk, but she dared not take them for fear of being discovered. The CIA team also built a perfect wooden box with Top Secret/Eyes Only stenciled on it. After a long discussion about what to name the fake alien operation, the CIA team agreed on M2, after the Robin Williams TV sitcom Mork and Mindy, in which he played a visiting alien. The Chinese, they calculated, would not get the joke.

Eileen was scared but eager to make up for her betrayal and stay in California, hopefully at the Lab. "This one time only, right?" she pleaded with Patty. "I'll do it if Carissa agrees." Carissa reassured her, "This is how you start your new life, Eileen. You can still be part of the team. You're not really stealing from Rell. Remember how you were talking about getting a PhD? Don't be scared. We will all be with you every step of the way." That was true. FBI and CIA surveillance teams would be close by watching every move.

The meeting on the Hornet went according to Patty's plan. Eileen drove to the old Navy base in Alameda, boarded the decorated Navy vessel, and spotted her contact immediately. The young Chinese woman was wearing a purple Patagonia fleece jacket and a yellow ribbon in her hair, as arranged. She was milling around on the lower deck in front of the famous Airstream trailer where astronauts Neil Armstrong, Michael

Collins and Buzz Aldrin stayed in quarantine until they were cleared to tell the world about the first walk on the moon. The two spies came face to face.

Eileen was stunned that her MSS contact looked strikingly like her. Same mid-length dark hair, the same slender body type, and a similar disarmingly friendly smile. "Hi Eileen," the MSS officer said and extended her hand in greeting. Eileen smiled back, shook her hand, and stood there staring blankly. "My name is Linda. I've been looking forward to meeting you. Shall we take a look around?" They strolled side by side past the antique airplanes and Apollo memorabilia to the fantail deck, which had a spectacular view of the San Francisco skyline. "Do you have a gift for me?" Linda inquired playfully. Eileen took off her green REI backpack and removed the sealed plastic bag containing the bogus relic. She handed it to Linda, who deposited the bag into a Hello Kitty lunch box. "I hope it's not radioactive," Linda jested. "Thank you, Eileen. I hope to see you again. Bye-bye for now." Eileen watched Linda walk breezily back through the exhibits, hips swinging, down the gangplank, and disappear from her view, but not from the trained eyes of the teams of FBI, CIA and probably MSS agents monitoring the handoff.

The FBI followed Linda as she walked from the Hornet a short distance to the Alameda Seaplane ferry landing, where she caught a ferry to Pier 39 and Fisherman's Wharf, transferred to a ferry going across the Bay to Larkspur, got into a Toyota Rav4 SUV parked in the commuter lot, and drove back across the Golden Gate Bridge into San Francisco, where she parked the Toyota in an underground garage on Clay Street, near Chinatown. In the parking garage, she switched her purple Patagonia for a black San Francisco Giants hoodie and hopped on a crowded cable car at the nearby California and Kearney Street station. "It's nice to see a little professionalism," special agent Medina commented cynically to Gabiera. They were part of the team that was tailing Linda, whose backtracking, appearance-changing and route-switching revealed her training as a professional spy. Posing as tourists on the cross-Bay ferries was easy, but they lost her when she picked up the car in Larkspur and doubled back across the Golden Gate Bridge. The CIA team used the hidden antennae in the artifact to track Linda's route back into the city, where she ditched the car and hopped on one of San Francisco's iconic cable cars. Linda knew what she was doing.

Medina and Gabiera took the Larkspur ferry back to Fisherman's Wharf and intercepted Linda as she hopped off the cable car at the California and Drumm Street station and set off on foot toward the Embarcadero. "I'm curious to see where she goes," Maya said to Gabriel. "The consulate is on Geary and Laguna, but I doubt she would be dumb enough to go there. They must have a safe house, or she's going to hand off the Hello Kitty lunch box to another agent."

Maya was right. Linda jumped off the cable car at the end of the line, walked down Market Street toward the Ferry Building, turned left onto the Embarcadero, back toward Fisherman's Wharf, heading straight toward Maya and Gabriel, who were walking toward her in the opposite direction, along the Embarcadero. But moments before they came face to face, Linda abruptly turned right into the Exploratorium, the hands-on science museum and learning center, where busloads of school kids from around the Bay Area converged on field trips to learn about science and nature.

The chaos provided the perfect cover for the hand-off. "Not bad," Maya observed. They followed her into the entrance, paid their admission, and lost her in the raging sea of pubescent children swarming around the whimsical science displays, with teachers yelling and museum curators straining to get their attention. What they did not see was that Linda made a beeline to the bathroom, where she handed the lunch box to a plump, middle-aged, heavily tattooed, Caucasian woman wearing a tie-dyed sundress and gray dreadlocks – straight out of Santa Cruz. The hippie chick stashed the lunchbox in her REI backpack, got into her 1998 Honda Accord that was parked in the lot across the street, and drove south on Highway 101 to the San Francisco airport, where she handed the backpack to an elderly Chinese woman who was waiting in the international departures drop off area. Within a few hours, the CIA tracked the object as it boarded a direct flight to Hong Kong. After the handoff at the Exploratorium, Linda had ditched her Giants hoodie in the bathroom stall and blended into the crowd with her hair in pigtails, Nike running shorts, stylish sunglasses, flip-flops, and an athletic running bra/halter top, all of which she was wearing under her previous disguise. Linda was gone, but the object was on its way.

CHAPTER THIRTY-FIVE

From Russia with Love

Andrei was miserable. Fresno sucked. "I hate this place, Carissa. It reminds me of India, but instead of curry, everything smells like tacos. My students are horrible. My apartment is next to the highway. I can't sleep. Why did you put me there? You have to get me out of this place. I want to come live with you, Carissa." He was a gifted physicist, no doubt, but also a big pain in the ass for Carissa and for the team working with him on how to use the Flow to evacuate space debris.

Andrei understood the Flow better than anyone. The energized particles flowed through the orbital domains like Carissa had theorized. The Russian experiments confirmed the existence of the exo-atmospheric rivers. The challenge now was to figure out how to artificially charge up the rivers with enough of the right kinds of energy to drag pieces of debris along with the Smoore currents. Andrei calculated that lasers could impart enough energy into the Flow to "light them up" like the Northern Lights and use the energy to sweep the particulates with the current out of Earth orbit, towards the stars. He was working with the laser experts at Livermore and the international Clean Sweep scientists on how to translate Flow theory into Flow practice. But he was miserable. And difficult. And lonely.

The big question was, how much energy would it take to illuminate the Smoore Flow phenomena? No single country possessed enough directed energy capacity to do the job, but the combined power of multiple countries might cross the photic excitement threshold.

"Don't cross the streams!" Rell joked to the international group meeting via video conference. "C'mon folks, it's from Ghostbusters Ghostbusters," they tried to explain. "Get w with the program, people."

Rell enjoyed giving the group tantalizing peeks at the wood box with the Top Secret stencil on her desk, shifting its position or removing it from view altogether. They put a new, nearly indistinguishable scratch on it to make the watchers wonder if it was the same box or a different one. How many boxes are there? Rell likened it to a shell game, where unsuspecting dupes bet money to find a hidden ball.

"Where are the ancient aliens today?" they quipped as they moved the box to a new location.

Eileen was now in on the joke and sharing in the fun of fucking with the foreign intelligence agencies who were desperately trying to sneak a peek at the mysterious boxes of alien goodies. She had taken the news of her deception graciously and was mostly just relieved to be initiated as a full member of the team, even if she was still under the watchful eyes of the FBI, CIA, and MSS. Rell had even invited her to move into her spare bedroom in Pleasanton as a peace offering, but the FBI insisted that she stay in the safe house they had arranged in Livermore, close to the lab.

Everyone understood the broader implications of the Smoore Flow phenomena. If it could be weaponized, it would torch anything in its path. But for now, it could also serve as a powerful symbol of international cooperation to solve a problem facing all of humanity: orbital pollution. It could also serve as a good collaborative starting point for the Artemis Accords. Scientists around the world enthusiastically shared insights into the new phenomena and designed experiments to test their hypotheses. The International Space Station provided a perfect venue from which to probe the undulating tentacles of the Flow. India led a series of BRICS alliance experiments to measure its effects on the moon. A joint U.S.-China-India-Russia experiment involved aiming multiple lasers into the Flow from a variety of ground stations and satellites.

"Don't cross the streams!" Rell exhorted, still with no response. "Ghostbusters, you idiots," they mumbled to their colleagues in the Livermore control room. Livermore's Duke modeling and simulation system was instrumental in providing orbital traffic management for the experiments, and Los Alamos' Oppie was essential for mapping and visualizing the swirling electromagnetic effects. Teams from around the world collaborated to build a complete picture of the Flow.

Andrei enjoyed lecturing his international colleagues and participating in video conferences on the physics of the Flow. He was brilliant and insufferable, not unlike many of his colleagues in the physics world, who didn't seem to mind his self-centered demeanor.

Sometimes, he would talk for an hour straight, scribbling calculations on a whiteboard with impossible-to-read markers with his back to the camera. But they knew genius when they saw it and took copious notes when he launched into his mathematical diatribes. His former Russian colleagues chafed as he ignored their contributions and took credit for their work. He missed Russia but knew he would never return. There was a growing consensus among the group that the Flow would have tremendous potential for planetary defense against rogue asteroids, which could be incinerated before striking Earth.

While the Flow was too far out in space to be used to zap ballistic missiles in the atmosphere, it was looking like it could be used as a shield against space-based weapons, especially those aimed at Earth, like a supercharged Van Allen Belt on steroids. Could the Flow reincarnate Ronald Reagan's Star Wars strategic defense shield? If a nuclear-armed country were able to bend the Flow to make itself invulnerable to attack, the fundamental principles of deterrence could be undercut. If a country could "light up" the Flow, it might also be able to fry enemy space systems. It might also be valuable for planetary defense against rogue asteroids—or space invaders.

Like the Manhattan Project scientists who thought the power of the atom should not belong to any single nation and favored entrusting

The Absolute Weapon to an international o organization, some of the Flow scientists began talking about international control of electromagnetic fifields surrounding the Earth. Andrei was one of them.

"Carissa," he urged, "We must not allow the Flow to become an instrument of state power. Can't you see that the Chinese, Russians, Indians, and even the Americans are preparing to harness its beauty to destroy one another? It must not happen."

"Andrei, I understand what you're saying, but that's way out in the future. Our job now is to understand the Flow and use it for good.

Don't be so dramatic."

"Carissa, I hate Fresno. I want to come live with you in Oakland. We should get married."

Carissa had zero interest in rekindling her affair with Andrei. His pathetic pleading and diarrhea incident in India had sealed the deal. There was no chance, but she felt sorry for him, alone in Fresno without friends or family. His only outlet was the international Clean Sweep community and he loved to lecture on the video meetings.

Maybe she could find him a girl. Eileen? No. Terrible idea. What about a lab scientist? How about Bianca Valenti? No, I think she likes girls. Maybe I should introduce her to Keala? No, another bad idea.

What about Kim Berringer? Maybe. She's cute and smart. Hell, she designs nuclear weapons. PhD from MIT, divorced, no kids. Likes hiking. I should introduce them when he comes to the lab for the next Clean Sweep meeting.

"I'm sorry you don't like Fresno, Andrei. It's close to the Sierras, and it's got a good football team but no hockey. I get it. That would be like me without baseball. Let me think about it. You hang in there, okay?"

"Maybe a bit longer, Carissa, but I have options, you know. I am internationally recognized and have received n numerous offers to take my research where I am appreciated. And my ideas."

"Oh yeah? Where would you go?"

"I have an offer—from India, at the Indian Institute of Technology in Bangalore."

"I thought you hated India?"

"I do, but I can't stay in Fresno, and I see that you do not love me. There's nothing for me here."

"I'm sorry, Andrei, but things have changed. Have you talked to the FBI or the CIA about moving to India?"

"I don't need anyone's approval," he snapped defiantly.

"Actually, I think you do, but let's not worry about that now. We all love the work you are doing on the Flow."

Andrei was not Carissa's biggest worry. She needed to talk to the president about the strategic implications of the Flow. But Andrei wasn't making things easy for her. He published a controversial article in the Bulletin of the Atomic Scientists opposing the weaponization of the Flow in which he accused the U.S. government of doing just that.

He gave a television interview in which he taunted the FSB as "a bunch of drunken losers" and described how the CIA had exfiltrated him from India. He stopped showing up to teach his classes and blew off meetings with his FBI handlers. One night, he showed up unannounced at Carissa's house at two in the morning, drunk and belligerent, to tell her that he had accepted the offer from India and would be leaving soon.

Carissa asked Patty what the CIA would do if Andrei tried to move to India.

Patty said, "It depends. Would he be willing to report on his research?

If he's working with Indian scientists, or Russians, or Iranians, we might be interested. Do you care if he leaves?"

"No, not at all," Carissa admitted. "It would actually be a big relief.

He showed up at my house the other night at two in the morning, drunk off his ass, and it scared the shit out of me. He's in love with me and wants to get back together, but it's not going to happen. So you guys are okay with him taking the job in India?"

Patty thought for a moment and said, "We can work with it. We might even be able to help. He's not doing anything for us here."

CHAPTER THIRTY-SIX

The Hotwash

A hotwash is where the participants in an operation gather to figure out what happened and assess what worked and what didn't. The group then writes an after-action report to share any lessons learned and recommend ways to improve future performance. CGSR Director Robert August hosted the Scorched Skies hotwash at Livermore Lab. Nearly 100 attendees representing USG agencies, the White House, the Defense Department, the intelligence community, Congress, the private sector, and partner nations gathered to assess future threats and policy options for the space domain.

Future threats included the risk of another Kessler event and the possibility of more Blossom Flower-type attacks on U.S. space assets. Nobody doubted that Russia and China would try again if they thought they could get away with it. The panels assessed the Quicksilver program, Lucky Slater's Silver Surfer, and the international Clean Sweep effort. One panel was dedicated to deterrence in space, and another focused on the implications of the Smoore Flow. The final panel would evaluate the emerging space architecture and the new global balance of power.

At the outset, the group acknowledged how prescient Carissa's wargame had been and that the insights gleaned from it should have been heeded. But that was water under the bridge. The group agreed that space was quickly returning to its pre-Kessler condition of being crowded, contested, and chaotic. There was no way to control the countries and companies rushing to repopulate the orbits and reap the benefits of space. The prospects for international cooperation were doubtful. The Artemis Treaty was good, but it had no verification and no enforcement. Most countries had agreed to the provisions for receiving assistance—no weaponization and adherence to the safety protocols in exchange for access to civilian space technologies, but that wouldn't stop cheating. Competing U.S., China, Russia, India and many other national and regional navigation and communications networks would make it nearly impossible to establish or enforce universal standards.

Space was going to be a rock'em, sock'em, Wild West, free market, free for all, with little governance. There would be no space Leviathan, no Galactic parliament, just like before. Not even a lawless society. So be it.

There was a broad consensus among the group that the United States had no alternative but to fortify its civil and military space capabilities across the board, especially if the U.S. expected to play a leadership role in the patchwork of emerging military and economic alliances that were already shaping the new world order. NASA would have to double in size. SPACECOM would have to build a space force that was ready to fight and win anywhere in the space domain, even if that meant doubling or tripling its budget. Same for the NRO and NGA.

There was simply too much at stake to leave it to chance. Sun Ra was ahead of his time when he said, "Space is the place."

To lead in the emerging multi-domain reality, America would have to improve its intelligence capability for strategic warning. "We should have known about the Blossom Flower plot," Reny Yater told the group. "How could they build and operate a secret moon base without us knowing? We have to up our game. Maybe it wasn't Pearl Harbor, but it was pretty damn close."

Lisa Owens, the National Intelligence Officer (NIO) for Space, added, "Building on what Reny is saying, we definitely need better technical assets in space to monitor the full range of adversary activities in the space domain, like what SPACECOM is doing with its space surveillance units, but we also need to prioritize all-source collection and analysis of national space programs down here on Earth.

We should be picking up information about their intentions as well as their technologies before they launch them into orbit. We can learn a lot from their S&T investments and their supply chains for space technology. There's a gold mine of HUMINT and SIGINT just waiting to be exploited. The Director of National Intelligence has already met with CIA Director Peterson to discuss establishing a new division for space HUMINT. We need to train a new generation of space-savvy case officers."

The group endorsed a major initiative to track the intentions and capabilities of international space programs, including raising the priority of space on the National Intelligence Priorities Framework (NIPF), the IC guide for apportioning spy resources. Stephanie Gilmore, the NSC senior director for space, addressed the group:

"Based on what I'm hearing, I'm ready to recommend to the president that we establish a center for all-source space intelligence. I think that we do it right here at Livermore, where we have the technical expertise, like Carissa's space tracking team, the National Atmospheric Radiation Advisory folks right next door, the nuclear weapons program, the laser experts, the computing power, and Z Program to make sense of it all.

Plus, Vandenberg is right down the road."

Rell kicked Carissa under the table and whispered, "Look what you did."

Dr. August chaired a panel on integrated deterrence, in which he explained the rationale for the new policy that the president had asked him to help draft. Each of the major components— conventional, nuclear, cyber and space—needed to stand on its own, but also had to fit together as a whole. The panelists from STRATCOM, SPACECOM, and CYBERCOM outlined their deterrence priorities. Then, Dr. August summarized in his commanding baritone.

"To solve the Rubik's cube of complex deterrence, our deterrence posture in each domain must be credible in its own right. And since modern conflict is not confined to specific domains, it is necessary to demonstrate cross-domain flexibility. Deterrence i is not domain-specific but interchangeable, according to the circumstances. I am not suggesting that we threaten to retaliate against a cyberattack with nuclear weapons, but our adversaries must know with certainty that we have the will and the capability to ensure that aggression against our vital interests in any domain will be met with a response that guarantees that they will fail to achieve their objectives. Integrated deterrence is more than the sum of its parts. It is a unified set of options designed to dissuade reckless risk-taking or careless miscalculation. The new policy makes our deterrence posture crystal clear."

Uncharacteristic for a policy workshop, August's statement received a standing ovation from nearly all of the participants. Seemingly unaware, Andrei checked his phone.

Lucky Slater chaired the next panel on public-private partnerships.

He started the session with a rant against China and Russia for triggering the Kessler Effect and concluded with an impassioned plea to "clean up the other trash in space like the filth and disinformation being spread by John Kramer and his financial backers." Lucky was an idealist at heart. Representatives from the big space launch providers raised eyebrows around the room with their descriptions of the unprecedented pace at which they were repopulating LEO with new payloads of every shape and variety. "Are you launching satellites for the drug cartels? Truth Social? How about Pornhub or the gambling syndicates?" Lucky asked cynically. "I noticed that wanker Kramer is already working for a Chinese broadcast company, helping them put up a new constellation to spread their lies and propaganda."

It was true that John Kramer was back to his old tricks, helping rogue Russian and Chinese oligarchs set up a global broadcast network specializing in pornography and gambling.

"I'm just giving the people what they want," Kramer explained in an interview. Would the reconstructed space architecture help humanity or indulge its worst instincts? Probably both.

The CEO of a small CubeSat company described t the obstacles that still made it fifinancially undesirable to work with the government. "I can't wait around for months to get answers," she complained. "We have to move at the speed of business to stay alive. With the demand the way it is, it's just not worth waiting around for government approvals." Government officials tried to reassure the skeptical audience that streamlined procedures and expedited procurement contract rules would cut through bureaucratic red tape. One company representative dismissed the new rules as "lipstick on a pig." Another commented that his company had founded a separate division to work with the government "so it doesn't infect the rest of the company with its slowness and secrecy."

Lucky asked the group, "How many of you from the private sector would agree to do a one-year assignment inside the government, to help with the new space policies?" A few interns raised their hands.

Nobody in the private sector wanted to take a pay cut and submit to government background investigations.

Andrei used the panel on the Smoore Flow to lecture the group on the dangers of allowing the Flow phenomena to be weaponized and

the need for international controls to prevent it from being hijacked for military purposes. Carissa presented her theoretical work that had led to the discovery of the Flow. An Indian scientist updated the group on the successful use of lasers to activate the Flow fifields for the purpose of incinerating space debris. The group lauded the international scientific cooperation that had made Operation Clean Sweep a success and vowed to expand cooperation to keep the orbits safe for scientific exploration.

In the final session, Carissa joined her old friend George Downing to describe the work of the president's expert panel on the strategy for an optimized satellite network that could help end poverty, provide limitless solar energy, boost education, and fuel economic development. They tried to hide their disappointment that the emerging satellite network was far from optimized for these purposes and that the expert report was taking forever. Ambassador Marks outlined the new Artemis Accords and described how they reinforced norms of behavior for a "free and equitable space domain."

Rell nudged Eileen, who was sitting next to her, and whispered, "Nothing about aliens?"

Eileen chuckled and replied, "We should have a whole panel on extraterrestrial life forms. I dare you say something."

Rell was not one to pass up a dare, and immediately raised their hand to ask a question. "Ambassador Marks, does the new treaty contain provisions to guide international cooperation for first contact with alien species?"

Ambassador Marks knew about the CIA operation to prank Chinese intelligence and was happy to go along with the joke. "Well, Dr. Sunn, we believe the principles embodied in the treaty are universal and would therefore apply to extraterrestrial interactions." Many in the room guffffawed. A few shook their heads in disbelief. With no Chinese or Russians in attendance at the workshop, it was left to Eileen to text her MSS handlers to inform them about the Ambassador's remark, which appeared to take seriously the prospect of alien encounters. She was having fun with her role as a double agent.

The CIA had tracked the fabricated alien orb to the same lab in Wuhan province where American analysts suspected the COVID-19 virus had originated. Sending it to a bio lab suggested they were searching for biological remnants, probably to sequence the DNA.

SIGINT reporting suggested that the Chinese scientists were skeptical of the objects' authenticity, but they were afraid to tell the MSS that the CIA had pranked them. So they kept quiet. Eileen kept texting tantalizing clues and fabricated information that the FBI traced to MSS instructions to other assets in the U.S. who had been tasked to collect information on extraterrestrial technologies.

The MSS directed one of its assets in Washington DC to make contact with a former Air Force intelligence officer who claimed to have knowledge of a super-secret alien technology program. With Eileen and Rell's help, the CIA planted more tantalizing tidbits of information for the MSS to discover, like rotten little Easter eggs.

Dr. August closed the hotwash session with a suggestion that Carissa should host another wargame to test out the new realities of space and global power. "We should give Lucky the do-over he asked for at the end of the previous wargame," he suggested.

Carissa grimaced. Here we go again, she thought. Just what I need.

Another wargame. But it would be interesting.

Later that night, the nerd squad gathered on Carissa's deck in the Oakland hills. The sounds of Earth, Wind, and Fire; the Isley Brothers; and Marvin Gaye echoed through the canyon as her friends shared stories about work, life, and the state of the world. Carissa inherited her musical tastes from her parents—lots of sixties R&B and soul, some reggae, and Bad Bunny. She loved Bad Bunny. Growing up on the outskirts of Washington DC, she also liked George Clinton's Funkadelic house music and the black punk rock band Bad Brains, but that was too much for this crowd. Carissa kept the vibe mellow and relaxed.

She invited her White House colleague Steph Gilmore and National Intelligence Officer Lisa Owens to join the party. They seemed friendly, but they had questions about the president. "Does she really like baseball, or is she just trying to take a break from the craziness of the White House?" Gilmore asked.

Carissa was wary about talking about the president, especially her personal life. "She really loves baseball, and she knows a lot about it," Carissa shared, cautiously. "Although, she's deluded about the Nationals. They really suck. So did my team, the Orioles, for a long time, but they're good now."

Owens asked, "What else does she like to talk about? She's so closed off and doesn't seem to have many friends or family, not being married and everything."

"We worry about her," Steph added.

Carissa replied, "She's pretty normal, but you're right about her being lonely. It's a lonely job. I think baseball is her escape. It's like that for lots of people, including me. I grew up with it. So did Keala."

"What about romantic interests?" Lisa probed, suggestively. "Does she have anyone? I know it must be hard, always being under the microscope, not fifitting into the standard model. Not married, no kids... We wondered if you two, you know...."

"Nah, it's not like that. She's lonely, for sure, and totally committed to her job. Maybe after she's done being president, she will find time for love. And for the record, I like men. You guys like red or white wine? I ordered pizzas."

As Carissa was going to the kitchen to get more wine for her guests, her Los Alamos counterpart Gerry Lopez caught her in the hallway. He looked better in person than on the video conferences; taller, with greenish eyes and bulging biceps wrapped in tribal Hawaiian tattoos.

Kind of a stud, actually. "Carissa, I was wondering, are you busy this weekend?" "Not really," she answered with a hint of coyness.

"Would you like to go hiking?" Lopez asked. "I'm here for the weekend and thought I would explore some of the trails around here,

in Joaquin Miller and Tilden Parks. I was wondering if maybe you would like to join me?" He was nervous. So was she.

"I know those trails pretty well," she replied. "My favorite in Tilden is the Seaview trail. It's a little over five miles, with spectacular views of the ocean." She thought to herself, What a dumb thing to say. Of course, it has views of the sea. It's the frigggging Seaview trail, for god's sake.

"How about tomorrow morning?" Gerry asked. "Around ten? I'll pick you up here."

"Sure, it's a date. Well, not a date, but sort of a date," she replied, self-consciously.

Walking to the kitchen, she thought I guess Rell was right that he's into in me. Well, we'll see what's up with that. The party gave everyone a chance to relax and unwind. Lucky offered Eileen a job at his company, which she declined, and then he asked her on a date, which she accepted. "I hope he doesn't expect me to go to space with him," she told Carissa. Andrei was in a much better mood since he had announced his departure to India and was regaling the group with stories about Russia's scientific accomplishments and KGB/SVR stupidity. Robert August shared a story about his encounter with a Grizzly bear on his latest backcountry adventure.

A group of lab scientists huddled in the corner of the deck to discuss recent developments in Smoore Flow research. Yater and Clark, now in the private sector and no longer restricted by government rules, shared a blunt with Lucky and jokingly blew smoke at their government colleagues, who were still subject to random drug testing.

"Hey, keep that shit away from me," complained a Z Program intel analyst.

"Blow it over here," Rell urged. "I can't wait until they get rid of that stupid rule. I'm going to get so fucking wasted."

The party lasted past midnight, which w was late for this group. A few people who drank too much crashed at Carissa's house, which had become the unofficial headquarters for the nerd squad that saved space. Gerry Lopez stayed to help Carissa clean up and put the trash and recycling in the right bins. As they were saying goodnight, he put his hands on her hips and gave her a quick kiss on the lips.

CHAPTER THIRTY-SEVEN

The Turning Point

Chairman Xi did not have much time to ponder celestial hairman phenomena like alien visitors. His country was ablaze. The economy had crashed, and violent protests were sweeping across the land. The bad loans and corruption that had killed the Belt and Road Initiative came home to roost as joblessness and food shortages across China spawned intense social upheaval. Foreign adventurism had not sparked the hoped-for surge of nationalistic pride, as Xi had imagined. Instead, violent protests wracked Hong Kong, Tibet, and Xinjang, and were spreading to the industrial mega-cities of Chengdu and Chongqing. Separatist and democratic leaders demanded freedom. Taiwan declared independence.

The Chinese people demanded better lives, not territorial conquests. Chinese workers were excluded from the booming space economy, as foreign investors shunned China's controlled markets and endemic corruption and turned instead to India, Africa, and South America to build less risky supply chains. As globalization devolved into an era of regionalism, Xi's grand plans to lead the world devolved into a desperate effort to cling to power. With no legitimacy and little to offer, the CCP was crumbling around him. Change was coming to the Middle Kingdom, and Xi knew he would not survive.

Throughout Asia, countries pushed back against China's territorial claims. Xi's navy was in retreat. Japan, the Philippines, Vietnam, Malaysia, and Indonesia sent warships to remove Beijing's structures from the disputed islands and artificial reefs that China had brazenly claimed. Japan and the Republic of Korea overcame decades of distrust to negotiate a bilateral defense pact. North Korea stood alone in supporting their communist benefactors, but it was just a matter of time before the aid pipeline from Beijing stopped flowing and the North Korean dictator would face his own domestic crisis.

South Korea started planning for regime change and the safe recovery of Pyongyang's weapons of mass destruction. American diplomats discreetly inquired what they planned to do with them.

There were also protests in Russia, but instead of economic prosperity, the Russian people demanded victory—victory over Ukraine, Poland, the Baltics, NATO, the U.S., Nazis, Jews, Muslims, capitalists, and the sexual deviants who they believed had been unleashed by the scourge of Western Liberalism. Putin had promised to restore the greatness of the former Soviet empire but had delivered little more than a series of embarrassing defeats and economic disasters that merely showcased Russia's decrepitude. Centuries of lies and propaganda, about their own history and the history of the world left the Russian people unprepared to face the reality of their situation. They demanded the respect that they thought the great Russian empire deserved but got only isolation, derision, and scorn from the rest of the world. Sanctions brought further misery as the few companies still doing business in Russia fled the crumbling, rotten remains of the Russian empire.

Spurred by the space economy, the rapid expansion of alternative energy sources—solar, wind, nuclear, and hydrogen—gutted the value of Russia's oil. Profits from the Russian gas station couldn't save Putin. The oligarchs plotted his demise, backing their favorite factions within the thugocracy. Some backed the GRU and the Army to prevail, others put their money on the KGB/SVR/FSB to survive the bloody contest for power that everyone knew was coming. Who would control the nuclear weapons? The knives were out. Anyone who could do so moved their money, yachts and mistresses to Cyprus and Malta, where they could still get EU passports and launder their stolen cash. Was there anywhere Putin could invade to give his people a victory? Moldova? The Arctic? The moon? That had not worked out so well. He was desperate and alone, and he feared for his life. "It's the damn Americans and their colored revolutions t that did this to me!" he raged.

After nearly 100 years of Communist rule, the Russian empire was imploding in the second phase of the unravelling process that started with the collapse of the Soviet empire in 1989-1991.

Breakaway districts in Vladivostok, Siberia, and Chechnya declared independence. Finnish and Dagestani separatists soon followed. Fighting erupted along disputed areas of the Russia-China border.

Comrade Xi refused to take Putin's calls; he was busy dealing with colored revolutions of his own. American diplomats warned their Indian counterparts against exploiting the chaos to renew their own festering border clash with China. The decline from peak China to CCP regime change came faster than anyone had predicted. Who would rule China? American diplomats discreetly reached out to Chinese technocrats and business leaders to discuss options for the future and to get assurances about the safety and security of China's nuclear arsenal.

India continued its zig-zag path to great power status. In a land renowned for its unmatched diversity, Modi and his Hindu nationalist BJP party continued to stoke religious intolerance. They also faced domestic challenges, especially in renewed calls for an independent Sikh homeland in Khalistan. However, the Indian economy skyrocketed the country into global prominence, especially its technology sector. The Kessler Effect had levelled the playing field in space and given India an opportunity to catch up with and surpass its rivals as a major space power. India's Belt and Road alternatives flourished as the world shifted away from China and relocated its global supply lines to India. Modi refused to abandon Putin's sinking ship and continued to prop up

Russia's sagging economy with sanctions-busting trade, especially cheap oil, but it wasn't enough to save Putin or Russia from their fate. Modi was already thinking about how to profit from Putin's demise. "Who's the colonial master now?" he joked.

India also continued to expand its trade w with China, despite also preparing to deter and fifight Beijing if necessary. India hedged its bets by joining both sides of the opposing regional blocs, simultaneously aligning itself with Russia and China in the anti-Western Shanghai Cooperation Organization (SCO) while also participating in the Quad, which was established to counter Chinese and Russian aggression. New Delhi joined with the BRICs to oppose the liberal world order but touted its growing ties with the United States and Israel. Which side was India on?

Further confusing its strategic direction, India continued to buy weapons from Russia. The incompatible systems, however, made it nearly impossible to coordinate joint operations with its land, sea, and air forces. Israeli avionics, for example, were not compatible with Russian air defense systems, like the S-300, S-400, and S-500. The mishmash of foreign and homemade weapons also made it nearly impossible for India to train and fight with foreign partners, including the Quad. For example, New Delhi's new Russian submarines poisoned India's participation in Western naval exercises, which required compatible communications networks, port calls, and crew exchanges.

Russia forbade the Indian Navy from allowing Americans to board the new nuclear submarines, and the U.S. Navy could not sync its fire control systems with the Russian equipment. The same was true for their new Russian fighter jets, which were designed to shoot down American and European aircraft. How effective would India's Russian weapons be against Russia or its ally China?

With an assortment of American, European, Israeli, Russian, and "Made in India" weapons, the Indian military found itself on an island, unable to communicate among its forces, much less its growing list of prospective partners. With no grand strategy to guide its evolving military, the whole was less than the sum of the parts. New Delhi's modest nuclear arsenal and ambiguous nuclear strategy added little to its disjointed conventional warfighting forces.

Even Pakistan, still floundering on the verge of failed state status but bristling with nuclear weapons, understood t that its increasingly powerful neighbor was militarily hobbled by its incompatible forces and lack of reliable allies.

With so many problems of its own, Pakistan's perennially floundering government showed no interest in antagonizing India. The Pakistan Army had its hands full, keeping the lid on terrorist groups and separatist hotspots in Baluchistan, Khyber Pakhtunkhwa, and Kashmir. They were also clinging to power.

India was stuck in the middle of the new world order, proudly maintaining its independence, adrift in a sea of shifting allegiances, with few friends and many frenemies. New Delhi's seat on the expanded UN Security Council and its new UN Space Center hardly compensated for its military isolation. Like Russia and China, the shadow of India's internal divisions loomed over its future.

Even in the perennially volatile Middle East, domestic instability outstripped foreign threats as a defining feature of the new world order. The space economy was opening new possibilities. Israel and its Abraham Accords partners (joined by Saudi Arabia and Egypt) took full advantage of the space race to advance their interests in the reimagined global economy. This group developed a plan with Gaza's post-Hamas leaders and the new centrist Israeli government to transform Gaza and the West Bank into a futuristic showcase for green infrastructure, renewable energy, and autonomous vehicles as part of a two-state solution. Ironically, the wars on the ground and in space had destroyed legacy infrastructure but, in so doing had created opportunities to start fresh. With Israeli technology and Saudi/Gulf State financing, along with the removal of Hamas terrorists from within their ranks, the future of the Palestinians was suddenly brighter. They, too could share the wealth being created by the new space economy.

Without Russia's military assistance, the Assad government of Syria collapsed, opening the way for democratic opposition groups to reassert their desires for freedom. Turkey followed India's strategy of trying to play all sides against each other to keep its options open, but its embattled authoritarian leader Recep Erdogan found himself instead facing economic isolation and a new wave of Kurdish nationalism. He had overplayed his hand with NATO, Russia, and China. Domestically, Kurdish nationalists seized the opportunity to reassert their dream of consolidating territory from Turkey, Iraq, and Syria to establish the independent nation of Kurdistan. Nobody could stop them.

The future did not look so bright for Iran's theocratic regime. With their allies Russia and China crumbling from within and their regional proxies Hamas, Hezbollah, and the Houthis running for their lives, the Iranian government faced boiling anger from within. The suppressed rage of the Iranian people could no longer be contained, especially among women and young people who had had enough of the mullah's sanctimony and corruption. Iran's military had wasted precious resources supporting Russia's failed invasion of Ukraine, and its notorious Revolutionary Guards (IRGC) and Quds Force groups saw their Hamas, Hezbollah, and Houthi proxies decimated by U.S., Israeli, Jordanian, and Egyptian special operations units. Lebanon reemerged from its long Hezbollah nightmare. The countries of the region had had enough of Iran's meddling in their affairs.

The time for regime change had come. Secret negotiations with Iranian opposition groups reached an agreement with the U.S., France, and Israel that a new democratic government would eliminate Iran's nuclear weapons and missile programs in exchange for Tehran's participation in civilian space programs under the Artemis Treaty.

The young leaders of Iran understood they needed jobs more than religion, nuclear weapons, and terrorism. The United States emerged triumphant from the historic inflection point. America's space technologies provided the catalyst for economic and political renewal and a rallying point for technological innovation around the world. The space economy opened the floodgates for entrepreneurs to apply emerging technologies to create entirely new business models. The new businesses extended far beyond just rebuilding the old systems and led to innovations in manufacturing, transportation, energy, construction, advanced materials, communications, entertainment, and, of course, defense and security, just as Carissa's White House expert commission had imagined.

Sun Ra was right. Space is the place. America's open markets and free trade policies nurtured startups in every corner of the globe. The space war had bound Americans back together, at least for the moment, and fostered previously unimaginable partnerships and collaborations. Beyond its borders, the reshuffling of world power had strengthened America's allies and added many new ones. Dispatching Communism to the ash heap of history was good for the world.

The new world order was far from perfect. Life in the international system was still "nasty, brutish, and short" for those who could not ensure their security through balancing or bandwagoning. The gap between rich and poor persisted. Borders were still contested.

Migrants still risked their lives to find opportunities. Social media still spread lies and disinformation. Multilateral treaties, laws, and institutions still depended on powerful nations for verification and enforcement. Nations did not turn their swords into plowshares. Some of the new alliances turned out to be unreliable, but others solidified to provide real security benefits. NATO and America's trusted Asian allies remained steadfast, although the Quad was still a work in progress due to India's ambivalence. For now, China and Russia have turned inward and suspended their aggression against their neighbors. America's revitalized deterrence posture established a foundation of stability, predictability, and credibility that nurtured the emerging global order.

History has a habit of veering off in unexpected directions. The scorched skies space crisis triggered a radical inflection point in world affairs. The India-China border war sparked a war in space that carried unanticipated consequences, much like the assassination of a little-known archduke sparked World War I and destroyed Europe's Old-World balance of power. The creative destruction of the Kessler Effect opened the door to the Fourth Industrial Revolution and inadvertently spawned a new era of national self-determination. Maps of the world would have to be revised. The scorched skies caused a global redistribution of power that unleashed a tidal wave of political and economic freedom. It wasn't the end of history, but it was the dawn of a new age.

CHAPTER THIRTY-EIGHT

Keep on Rocking
in the Free World

Gerry and Carissa hiked the Seaview trail in Tilden Park. They kissed at the scenic viewpoint overlooking the San Francisco Bay and the Golden Gate Bridge. Afterward, they had lunch at the Yellow Door Café near her house in Montclair and talked about work, life and baseball. Gerry grew up in Los Angeles and was a Dodgers fan. Carissa hated the Dodgers, but at least he liked baseball. His dad came from Mexico and his mother was Samoan, hence the tribal tattoos to honor his mother's family. He went to Cal State Long Beach as an undergraduate, got his master's in engineering from the University of New Mexico, and took a job at Los Alamos National Lab designing experimental equipment. Gerry invited Carissa to an Isotopes game in Albuquerque, which she happily accepted. "When you come to New Mexico, we can hike Sandia Peak or in the Caldera National Preserve," he said. Carissa was smitten, but she had to return to Washington on Monday.

The president trusted Carissa and relied on her for advice on a wide range of issues, including topics that were way beyond her expertise. "Carissa, what do you think about flying cars? Is that realistic?" "Carissa, does methane from cows really contribute to climate change?" "Carissa, can you explain the difference between fission and fusion?" "Carissa, why do people think vaccines cause autism?" The president would invite Carissa to the White House for long discussions about everything from social justice to the emerging world order. They joked about pranking the CCP and speculated about the results of regime change in Russia and China. Was it possible that democracy would replace authoritarianism?

One result of the regime change t that was consuming Russia and China was growing concern about the safety and security of their nuclear weapons. Who would have their fingers on the nuclear button? Dr. August at Livermore urged Carissa to advise the president to launch a new and expanded Cooperative Threat Reduction (CTR) program to deal with loose nukes around the world. This was not the first time the U.S. government had rendered assistance to ensure that nuclear weapons and materials were safe and secure; after the Cold War, the U.S. had guaranteed the safety and security of nuclear, chemical, and biological weapons scattered throughout the territories of the former Soviet Union. The new effort would quietly reach out to military leaders in Russia, China, and elsewhere to offer U.S. assistance to help them secure their nuclear weapons and materials. The president agreed and asked Carissa to lead the effort, but she declined. She wanted to go home.

President Kennelly's first term in office would end soon, and she was busy campaigning for reelection. Carissa was not interested in politics and told her friend Keala that she planned to return to LLNL. "Carissa," the president pleaded, "I need you. Nobody else gives me straight answers like you. Who can I trust to lead the CTR program?"

"You have lots of good people at DOE, DOD, and State, Keala.

Besides, you can call me any time and I promise I'll give you my honest opinions about anything, except about the Nationals. You're delusional about them. They need a total rebuild. It's a shit show."

"I just like having you around, girl," the president said.

"Thank you, Madam President, for your trust and friendship. I've learned so much from you.," Carissa replied.

"We're not done yet, Carissa," said Keala. "Just wait and see. After the election."

Carissa's friends were thrilled to have her back home in California. Rell had stepped up to manage the space team while she was away and had discovered that they enjoyed the new responsibilities. Eileen was working undercover as a double agent for the FBI and the CIA, passing bad information and planting bogus items for her MSS handlers to discover. She was having regular meetings with Linda, the local MSS agent who she met on the USS Hornet. One new plot involved falsified research to use the Smoore Flow to communicate with interstellar visitors. Eileen was dating Lucky, who had offered to use his company to support the ongoing FBI and CIA operations.

Reny Yater, whose orbital tracking company was spectacularly successful, joked that the three of them—Rell, Eileen, and Lucky—" made a great thruple."

"You're a sick and twisted man," Lucky replied.

"I wish it were true," Rell added. Nobody knew if Rell was serious or not.

"What's a thruple?" Eileen asked.

They were all happy to have Carissa home. Before leaving Washington DC, she had persuaded her mother to come live with her in the Oakland hills. Fannie Moore had retired from teaching high school science in Baltimore and was lonely. She fifit right in with the nerd squad and enjoyed sipping chardonnay and listening to music with the gang hanging out on Carissa's deck. Now, she just needed to persuade Gerry Lopez to transfer from Los Alamos to Livermore.

He was a California boy, after all. Carissa agreed to lead Livermore's space program and turned leadership of the space situational awareness team over to Rell.

The new deterrence policy involved modernizing the ancient Cold War nuclear weapons infrastructure for the Fourth Industrial Age. Livermore was thriving. The U.S. had enough highly enriched uranium and plutonium but needed to replace t the antique weapons and the methods of fabricating them with modern techniques such as 3D printing, additive manufacturing, and AI design. Experimental equipment like the National Ignition Facility (NIF) at Livermore and the Dual Axis Radiographic Hydrodynamic Test (DARHT) facility at Los Alamos provided insights into the inner workings of nuclear weapons that made explosive tests unnecessary. The updated nuclear enterprise would ensure that a reimagined arsenal would be "fit for purpose" and flexible enough to adapt to changing geopolitical conditions. The three nuclear weapons labs, Livermore, Los Alamos, and Sandia, and the entire government nuclear enterprise were working overtime to design and build new weapons for the next generation of delivery systems, including a variety of hypersonic vehicles capable of operating in the region between space and the upper atmosphere. The new era of complex, multi-domain deterrence had arrived.

The Quicksilver, Silver Surfer, and international Clean Sweep efforts, combined with the massive program to repopulate the space domain, energized Livermore's space programs. The next generation of satellites employed the latest innovations in materials science, sensors, optics, and quantum communications, much of which was based on R&D done at LLNL. The Silent Barker replacements utilized these advancements to transform America's space-based intelligence, surveillance, and reconnaissance capabilities. Carissa's space situational awareness team quadrupled its budget and could still barely keep pace with the demands from SPACECOM and NRO to navigate through the still crowded but, for now, less contested skies.

George established a new division at NRO to use America's upgraded space capabilities to support scientific and humanitarian programs.

He was determined to seize the opportunity to use America's space dominance for the betterment of humanity. The top priority, however, was to restore America's eyes and ears in space with the new maneuverable, hyper-networked, secure, and resilient satellites.

In addition to their military, intelligence, and scientific missions, the government's new space assets were designed to deter attacks and defend, if necessary, the critical civilian space infrastructure that was advancing at breakneck speed. SPACECOM was going on offense. On the diplomatic front, the Artemis Accords provided a blueprint for space governance that nobody challenged, at least not yet.

The pace of discovery in science and technology accelerated like the rockets that were thrusting the new generation of satellites into orbit. The Smoore Flow revealed new insights into the solar system and the unseen connections between its planetary family members.

Charged particles were migrating around the planets on following flumes, like the Small World ride at Disneyland. Several countries launched research programs to determine if the Flow could be weaponized.

Carissa was the keynote speaker at several conferences devoted to research on the Flow. That's where she saw Andrei, who was delivering a paper on his new research on the Flow, which he was conducting in India. He had recovered a bit of his old swagger.

During a coffee break, he told her that his Indian wife was pregnant and that they were planning on returning to Russia. "Does Patty know about your plans?" she asked.

"Yes, it was her idea," Andrei replied. "My old institute wants me back. I'll be the director."

"That's great, Andrei. I'm happy for you," Carissa said.

Candidly, she thought it sounded like a train wreck waiting to happen, but it wasn't her problem. Besides, it might be good to have a source inside Russia's premier research institute. She enjoyed the spy stuff.

Gazing at the night sky from her d deck, Carissa felt pretty good about her life. She had good friends, meaningful work, and a loving family. What more could she ask? For the Orioles to win the World Series? Could happen. Even her romantic prospects were promising. As she pondered the cosmos, the International Space Station (ISS) tracking app on her phone alerted her that the ISS would soon be visible as it passed over the Bay Area. Somehow, the ISS had survived. She wondered who was up there tonight. Lucky and his dog? She was even looking forward to hosting another war game. Carissa had a new appreciation for the space domain and what it meant to keep it safe. They had a second chance. She hoped humanity wouldn't blow it. Hopefully, everyone understood how fragile it was and how easily it could all be ruined.

The darkness of the scorched skies gave way to a dawn of cautious optimism. Deterrence provides the foundation of stability on which peace and prosperity depend. That stability requires mutual acceptance of certain boundaries on conflflict. Rejection of those boundaries led to war, as it did for China, India, and Russia. Now that those boundaries had been reestablished among the major powers, peace was possible. The establishment of deterrence in space would extend those boundaries skyward to provide the stable ground needed for the seeds of prosperity to grow.

About the Author

Dr. Zachary Davis is a Senior Fellow at the Center for Global Security Research at Lawrence Livermore National Laboratory. He has broad experience in intelligence and national security policy and has held senior positions in the executive and legislative branches of the U.S. government.

Davis is the author of numerous government studies and reports on technical and regional proliferation issues. His scholarly publications include articles in *OrbisOrbis, Asian Survey, Arms Control Today, Security Studies, Arms Studies, The Nonproliferation Review, The American Interest,* and chapters in numerous edited volumes.

He was the editor of The Proliferation Puzzle: Why States Proliferate and What Results and The India-Pakistan Military Standoff. His edited volumes on Strategic Latency and World PowerPower were published in 2015, 2018 and 2020. His latest book is a techno-thriller about space warfare. He got his undergraduate degree at the University of California at Santa Cruz. Moreover, Davis holds doctorate and master's degrees from the University of Virginia. He enjoys surfing and tai chi.